NICHE
Internet
Marketing™

"The secrets to exploiting untapped niche markets
and unleashing a tsunami of cash -
while you kick back and relax."

NICHE Internet Marketing™
Leigh Burke

Design and Layout
Rusdi Saleh (fresh ideas!)

For those with the courage to transcend their place in this world.

For those of you living the dream that took the time to contribute to this book , thank-you.

To my loved ones and friends who inspire me every day.

Contents

Introduction

"Let us welcome controversial books
and controversial authors."

John Fitzgerald Kennedy

Welcome to the **Niche Internet Marketing book / course!**

There is a good reason I call this product both a book and a course. When you first go through the material, you will be learning as you go. I take you from the very basics, through to very advanced cutting-edge techniques. I highly recommend that you try out and apply my principles as you work your way though the material. In this respect, what you have purchased is a course. On the flipside, due to the miracle of the internet, I am able to deliver valuable additional material directly to you and your PC. Therefore, you what you have received is a publication in the format of a book, that directs you to electronic sites on the internet. The way I have designed Niche Internet Marketing has been to give you all the information you need from A-Z, so you will be able to use it as a reference you can turn back to again and again as you develop your internet businesses. All the links within this book are live websites, so you can go straight to the resources or tools you need by typing the URL into your favourite web browser. The contents pages, and index at the end make it easy to find what you are looking for throughout this book.

The information you are about to be made privilege to, is the sum of countless hours of research spent trawling through all the different methods available to an inexperienced and cash poor Website Marketer. The result is the cumulative experience gained from over 12 years spent in the industry. I have invested tens of thousands of dollars on every conceivable product and service in the pursuit of the ultimate Niche Internet Marketing strategies. I have even tried all the free products and services too!

So what is **Niche Internet Marketing?**

The definition of Niche Internet Marketing itself implies a number of certain traits of both the Internet Marketer, and the Internet Marketing campaign.

niche
n. 1. an ornamental recess in a wall or the like, usually semicircular in plan and arched, as for a statue or other decorative object.
2. a place or position suitable or appropriate for a person or thing: to find one's niche in the business world.
3. a distinct segment of a market.
adj. 4. pertaining to or intended for a market niche; having specific appeal: niche advertising.

in·ter·net
n. a vast computer network linking smaller computer networks worldwide (usually prec. by the). The Internet includes commercial, educational, governmental, and other networks, all of which use the same set of communications protocols.
mar·ket·ing
n 1: the exchange of goods for an agreed sum of money [syn: selling, mer-

chandising]

2: the commercial processes involved in promoting and selling and distributing a product or service; "most companies have a manager in charge of marketing"

A niche is any tightly focused segment of a market, having specific appeal. For example rather than selling containers or even buckets, or even red buckets, you might specialise in selling SMALL red buckets. That would be your niche. And if anybody wanted a small red bucket, they would know to come to you, because you are the expert and have the best stock for that particular niche.

Internet Marketing covers all the new marketing methods that have evolved online as the internet has expanded through all areas of our life. These include SEO (search engine optimisation), link building, article writing, email marketing, Adwords, YouTube marketing, Facebook marketing, list building and many other methods that are both black hat (illegal), grey hat (of dubious origin), and white hat (perfectly legal).

A niche internet marketer has entrepreneurial qualities. They can spot a trend, and use their skills to quickly create a product and site to take advantage of the demand and monetise the opportunity. They may have tens of sites or hundreds of sites. Each site may be earning them only a modest income, but the sum of all the multiple streams of income add up to produce a significant cashflow running on auto-pilot for the most part.

The internet has changed the way consumers consume. In his book "The Long Tail", Chris Anderson explains how the internet has created a unique culture of endless choice, and unlimited demand. This has created a "Long Tail", whereby it is no longer economically viable for the big conglomerates to chase the mega-hits (Top 10 music, best selling books, this seasons must-have product), as the bulk of sales has shifted to items that may only sell one unit a month. It is the sum of all these sales that for the first time in history has surpassed the high volume items and created a whole new market for niche products.

Niche Internet Marketing aims to give you the skills required to recognise, research and take advantage of opportunities as they arise. You are about to learn how to quickly and effortlessly create websites for your niche markets and monetise them before setting and moving onto your next opportunity. Over time, you will build up a network of niche product and service offerings that will bring you multiple streams of income providing extra income and / or freeing up your time.

With your extra income, you may buy the car you always wanted, or the house of your dreams. You might take an extra vacation every year. You may wish to escape the 9-5 all together and like Tim Ferriss the author of "The 4-Hour Work Week" join the new rich and take mini-retirements. Niche Internet Marketing can help you achieve those dreams.

Now if you are like me, you entered this Internet Marketing game, for the lure of great riches, with just a small outlay of both cash and time. Just like a modern-day gold rush! Now, the majority of us that have been involved in any type of Internet Marketing will know that to a degree, the afore-mentioned scenario is not necessarily always the case, and in fact is quite rare. Don't get me wrong, there are riches to be made in Internet Marketing, just like any other business, but it would be unwise to subscribe to the premise that all these riches and glory could be achieved overnight. Fortunately, with the right knowledge, some energy, motivation, focus and patience, what you can achieve will positively astound the average person on the street!

So back to what I was saying, being a Niche Internet Marketer is about doing things the smart way. Using the technology at our disposal to our advantage, and being intuitive, persistent, inquisitive, and resourceful. You will need to maximise the returns for your investment of time and money. The Niche Marketer will be one step ahead of the trends and will learn all the best technologies and methods for marketing their site. The Niche Marketer will also know the best products and services to sell online, what people are searching for, and what their needs are. Do you know what products are going to be the best sellers next Christmas? The Niche Marketer does! By researching, testing, and remaining focused and inquisitive, the Niche Marketer learns all the best ways of doing things. Knowledge is what gives the Niche Marketer his power, Internet Marketing Programs and Services are the tools of his trade.

If you have a good idea, with the correct application of my principles you stand to make a lot of money for yourself, and to live the lifestyle you always dreamed of. That is what I believe Niche Internet Marketing has to offer the average guy on the street, as well as small, medium and large businesses alike;

and that is choice. When you take the time and effort to put the systems in place, eventually you will reap the rewards of your efforts. This will provide cashflow, thus providing you with the luxury of choice. Choice to invest further in other businesses, spend some time holidaying with your family, or to purchase that vintage car you have always wanted, and drive down the coast. You see, your investment in time and effort up front, will ensure that you reap the rewards 3, 6 and 12 months time from now. An internet website business is like any other business though, you will still need to keep an eye on things, tweaking your business processes, marketing campaign, product and service offerings here and there, but for the most part, your business should be on auto-pilot, leaving you to enjoy the lifestyle you choose.

"So what is Niche Internet Marketing anyway?", I hear you ask. "And when are we going to get into the stuff which can help me become a real success?". Patience my friend, we're about to begin the journey in a moment. Just a few notes about the format of this book. If you are an experienced Niche Internet Marketer, some chapters, like Page Structure and Site Structure, may be a bit elementary for you. I have not included these simply to beef up the page count of this course. Each chapter is there for a very specific reason. I wanted this course to be an exhaustive reference for starting, running and marketing a successful Niche Website Business. There will be a lot of newbies reading this, and I want them to have an understanding of the full end-to-end process. In the Domain Names chapter, for instance, I have included considerations for when purchasing a domain name. I also include references to the particular sites and services I use where possible, to ensure newbies are not getting ripped off, and they are aware and able to access all the features they need. (Such as an admin panel for domain names.)

So who is Leigh Burke anyway? And what makes me qualified to teach Internet Marketing techniques? I started out in the Internet Marketing business 12 years ago when I was fresh out of university. Initially I marketed my own Websites. I then moved into web design, project management and eventually ended up where I am today as a consultant. I decided to put all my eggs in one basket and apply what I had learnt and just go for it. A couple of handfuls of successful sites later (and a few more in the pipeline), and I decided to teach what I have learnt, so others could benefit from my knowledge and experience. Anybody can write a book and put it on a website and try and sell it. The real challenge is getting people to see your site and make them interested in buying what you have to offer. So to me this was the ultimate challenge. Using my techniques to market an information product about my techniques! Well, you're reading this, so I must be doing something right!

In fact, I'd like to share an anecdote with you. Whilst researching and developing this book, I was simultaneously developing the website and sales copy that would eventually be used to market and sell the book online. After a few months, to my amazement sales started coming in for the book! Now I had done no marketing for the book, website or domain name. The domain name was fresh and had not been used before and had no incoming links. I had not submitted the domain name to any search engine or directories, and had not released details of the book or website to anybody! Eventually I had to take the home page down and send refunds and apologies to all those who had made a purchase, and offer them a discount when the product was finally released. But this story illustrates the power of the internet, even without Internet Marketing!

So there we have it. Get buckled up, sit back in your seats and hold on! Here goes..........................

Yours in success and happiness,

Leigh Burke.

Action item! >>>

> Go to your PC now and create a 'Niche Internet Marketing' folder in My Documents or on your desktop.

> You will use this folder to download free software and tools that I recommend throughout this book.

> Find a quiet room with no distractions, sit down, clear your mind of everything else and get ready to absorb Niche Internet Marketing.

Chapter 1

A brief history –
The internet and internet marketing, where it has come from.

> "I have but one lamp by which my feet are guided,
> and that is the lamp of experience. I know no way of judging
> of the future but by the past."
> Edward Gibbon

The internet itself has been around in one form or another since the late 70s. Originally it was designed by the military as a primitive way of sending encrypted messages intended only for their recipients. If you have ever used an electronic bulletin board, well this was similar, only networked.

Eventually, as most military applications do, the internet made its way into mainstream civilian application. The concept of the Internet, or the Web as it was sometimes also referred to as, didn't really take hold on the public psyche until the late 80s. That incarnation of the internet was somewhat slow, cumbersome and limited by both the number of sites available, and the cost of registering a domain name and hosting a site. With the advent of cheaper hosting and the reduction of the cost of registering domains, the popularity of the internet really started to take off in the early 90s. The media jumped on the bandwagon, and so ensued what was something of a mini cultural revolution.

Companies started registering domain names and setting up what were mainly informational web sites, or sales jargon online if you like. The real problem is that people only really knew about a website by reading the address from some offline source such as a sales brochure, business card or advertisement. When the consumer went to the site, they were presented with little more than they could get by reading the real world glossy paper brochure.

Along came the search engines to solve the problem of finding web sites amongst the vast majority of sites which were popping up on the internet all around the world. The original search engines were quite clunky, slow and easily manipulated. Various spamming methods were adopted by the less scrupulous web site owners to modify the results shown by the search engines. Tricks such as repeating the keyword name over and over again at the bottom of the html page, and then changing the font to white were often adopted, as well as copying the same page over and over again and linking them all together to boost a sites ranking.

Search engines soon cottoned on to these methods, and eventually the majority of them were filtered out. For the most part, databases were not very clean, and this combined with the suspect (but evolving) algorithms left the majority of the public disenchanted, and genuine website marketers scratching their heads at how to tweak their sites, and what to expect next. The searching public were yet to see a search algorithm that they were more than happy with.

Various companies such as yahoo.com and dmoz.org tried to circumvent the search conundrum by creating indexes of categorised, human approved web sites. For a while these proved quite popular, but were very difficult to get listed in, and required the directory companies to employ an army of developers, moderators and approvers to keep the directory running and clean. Of course, some of these were paid, but the majority were volunteers. So considering the limited results that could be obtained from a directory, the searching public seemed to employ a combination approach when conducting their searches, of both directories and search engines.

It was at this time, that search engine and directory companies started merging and acquiring competitors via takeover, as the forecasters must have seen the benefit of having a combination of both search and directory (and less competitors!) It was also around this time, that many engines and directories started charging for guaranteed paid inclusion. The future looked dim. It was at this time that a newcomer to the scene decided to take their chances with a newly created algorithm. Yes, Google was here! To the rest of the world, this must have seemed like an insane time to be entering the market. And a free search engine at that, with free submission for your site! But once Google started to increase in popularity, people saw the benefit of their superior algorithm and search results, nice uncluttered home page, and free submission, and hey, Google just sounds so cool anyway! The term to "google it" is now commonly used in relation to doing a search, and it seems the public can't get enough. Google has been innovative in other areas of the industry also. They have several indexes based on different topics, and some news archive services. Another innovation Google implemented was picture search. Google did go on to implement paid inclusion via AdWords and AdSense, but basic submission to the index has always been free. Google's spider also seems to be the most active, and often times linking to a new site from an older site which is already indexed will often get the new site indexed more quickly than if you submitted the site manually to Google.

Recent happenings in the world of search include Microsoft's MSN search which has recently been released after an extended BETA testing stage. On initial testing of the service, it seems to be quite robust and give good output. Microsoft's foray into search was meant to cause great waves, and rumours were that Google were dreading the day it was finally released. But in my opinion, unless they come up with something more innovative, such as Google has and continues to do, at this point they are not much of a threat. The only threat I foresee in the future, is if Microsoft hard codes the search page into Internet Explorer, but I don't see this happening, as consumer groups and the government's anti-competition lawyers would be down on them in a flash. So in the search arena, I guess we'll just have to wait and see, but in the meantime, it is wise to be tweaked and indexed for both Google and MSN search.

Google also recently shook up the free email market with their first offering called Gmail. Gmail is a free internet based email service offering users a 1GB account, and new search capabilities within the system itself. At the time of writing Gmail is still in beta testing stage, but with Google's initial announcement, Microsoft and yahoo quickly countered and increased the limit of their previously measly offerings. Once again, I guess we'll have to watch this space.

At the time when search engines were first being introduced to the internet, and the first primitive indexes, directories and listings compiled, a variety of internet marketing gurus started to appear on the scene. At first, the majority of these marketing experts were simply marketing people who had made their way from the real paper-based world to the electronic world of bits and bytes that is the internet. Marketing methods promoted often included a heavy slant towards sales copy, colours and formatting of your web site appearance, and then eventually submission to all the directories and search engines which started to appear around the net. These gurus also promoted the use metadata, keywords and other elements within the html. Eventually we were subjected to the unsightly and annoying barrage of spam email which internet marketers promoted. Fortunately for the internet marketing gurus, they also had the rights to distribute the software required for their clients to send mass email and make millions! (sic)

Most recently we have seen the rise in popularity of Web 2.0 sites such as www.YouTube.com, www.MySpace.com, www.FaceBook.com, and many many more. These sites are based around the concept of social networking, and are a very exciting development for the internet and internet marketers. Social networking allows users of these sites to build social networks based on pre-defined specifications in the member profile you create when you sign up. This has enormous power, and allows people to be profiled and potentially marketed to based on their profiles.

YouTube has made streaming video at no cost to the producer an actual reality. Finally real video content can be produced, uploaded and shared with the world. This has many exciting applications for the Niche Marketer.

In the internet's infancy, Internet Marketing itself was a niche. Not many people or companies were aware of the power of optimizing a website for the search engines, and indeed not many quality search engines themselves existed. Big websites such as Ebay and Amazon had to rely on offline advertising, media exposure and word of mouth. Amazon in particular was one of the earliest examples of a successful affiliate program where they had tens of thousands of other sites promoting their services for a cut of the profit.

Corey Rudl and the Internet Marketing Centre was one of the pioneers of Internet Marketing offering information products, expert tips, and seminars to teach people his methods. Sadly Corey died in a car racing accident in 2005, however his legacy lives on at http://www.marketingtips.com or www.internet-marketing.com.

Over the ensuing years, many other gurus came out of the woodwork, some fresh-faced from college, others having made the transition from offline 'marketing guru' status to 'internet marketing guru.' Often these guys and gals were pioneers making up methodologies and tools and testing them as they went along. As the debate raged amongst this ever-growing group of peers as to what was white hat (legal) and black hat (illegal or unethical), Google was often the final arbitrator – banning any sites that broke the rules. A list of all the current internet gurus can be found here: http://www.gurudaq.com

Finally we made it to where we are today. But where are we? And where are we headed? Read on, and you'll find all my predictions for the future, and the most absolute up to date, complete list of tools, tips and resources that I think you should be using right now, today, to be successful.

And don't forget to check at the end of this book for my list of resources to help you on your way to Niche Internet Marketing success.

Action item! >>>

> Go to the WayBackMachine: http://www.archive.org/index.php

> Enter 'Hotmail.com' and click 'Take me back'.

> Click on the different dates to view how Hotmail has changed throughout the years!

> Enter another favourite site and view older versions of the website.

Chapter 2

The future –
The future of internet marketing. Where is the industry headed, and how you can take advantage of this.

> "When it comes to the future, there are three kinds of people:
> those who let it happen, those who make it happen,
> and those who wonder what happened."
> John M Richardson Jr.

Shouldn't we all be flying around in spaceships by now? I don't know about you, but I was a massive Star Wars fan and Trekkie. I loved the technology, that's why I got into computers in the first place. So why hasn't technology taken over the world? Where is my lightsaber, speeder bike and portable comms unit? Look around you my friends, the future IS here!

Do you own a mobile phone? A laptop? PDA? Do you have a broadband connection? Does your car have fuel injection? Traction control? Satellite navigation? Do you pay your bills online? Do you have an email account you use for business or to keep in touch with loved ones?

History and future generations will look back on TODAY as a golden age. A time of great opportunity when fortunes were made and lost, and new social practices implemented. You often hear the term information age used to describe the current time in which we live. But it is only growing, and opportunity abounds for the entrepreneurial person who reaches out and grasps the opportunities before them.

Do you have a product or service which you sell offline? Could this product or service be marketed and sold online, thus expanding your potential customer-base exponentially?

Do you have an idea, special skill, story idea or song which you could make into an electronic document and market on the internet? The market and opportunities for people with creative ideas is so large these days, that the rules that once bound such pursuits have changed forever.

Here is my list of what I believe to be the big markets in the coming 10 years:

- Information Technology Security based products and services
- Energy saving products and services.
- Environmentally friendly based products and services.
- Entertainment based products.
- Health and fitness based products and services.
- Beauty based products and services.
- Life coaching based products and services.
- Investment based products and services.
- Holiday/vacation/Travel based products and services. (airfares, accommodation)
- Convenience based products and services (ie. Online grocery shopping, online ticket purchases, online bill payment, online vouchers.)
- Community based products and services (ie. Chatrooms, forums, email groups, all of these both wireless and online)
- Wireless products and services (ie. SMS, WAP, mobile ringtones, picture messaging, mobile chat, wireless gaming., wireless ticketing, wireless fee-based services like paying parking fees with mobile/cell phone, using mobile or cell phone to pay bus and train tickets, using mobile/cell phone to access vending machines.)
- Radio wave products (ie. There is a new technology called RFID (radio frequency identification. Currently RFIDa) used to track products from production to sale. This technology may have other applications.)
- Education based products and services (ie. Online learning, access to electronic documents for study purposes.)
- Video over net.
- Internet based Telephony products and services. (Skype)
- Telecommuting products and services.
- Integration based products and services (ie. Getting all your products

and services through one supplier. Eg. Landline phone, mobile/cell (including sms and wap), gaming, movies on demand, internet, digital tv, cable tv. OR a bank account with credit card, house loan, personal loan, share investment portfolio, insurance)

- All in one devices (ie. a cell/mobile phone with a colour camera, gaming device, pda, mp3 player, radio, and ticketing device. OR TV, video on demand, internet, music system.)
- Internet enabled housing (ie. switching lights and appliances on remotely, monitoring security over the internet via alarms and video. Fridges ordering milk and butter. Automatic vacuum systems able to be activated remotely.)
- Products and services marketed towards China, India and Indonesia.
- Products and services provided from China, India and Indonesia to the rest of the world.
- Services that can provide integration between the developing, fledgling superpowers of the East and the West.
- Miniaturised mass storage devices and backup solutions.
- Cheap, lightweight portable computing devices.
- Mass storage MP3 players. (iPod)

When choosing your market, you should aim for the narrowest field in that segment as you can. Rather than choosing to market a music site, target a particular genre such as Jazz Music. Rather than create a generalist sports site, focus on Baseball.

Whatever product or service you choose to target as your niche, remember to aim for the long tail. It may not be low-hanging fruit, but boy when you get your hands on it – it certainly is sweet and tasty!

Remember the era of the hit is coming to an end. With endless choice and accessibility, consumers will no longer gravitate towards generalist categories in the market place. Consumers will research online and hone in on the specific product or service that delivers EXACTLY what they want. Fulfil these niche opportunities and you will be on the road to achieving your business and personal dreams.

So there we have it. My list of what I predict to be the big ticket item product and services in the coming years. If you have any further ideas or thoughts for what you think the future holds, email them in and I will include them in my next edition. The above is all subjective of course, but if you pay close attention, you can figure out where the trends are heading and take advantage of the opportunities new technologies present, and the new markets that they open up. The keen eyed Niche Internet Marketer will be on the lookout for these opportunities, and seize them when they arise. So keep your eyes peeled, and ear to the ground.

Action item! >>>

> Go to the Google's Technology News site: http://news.google.com/?ned=us&topic=t

> View some articles on the latest Technology Trends

> Bookmark this and other technology news sites and visit them daily!

Chapter 3

What to do now –
What you should do right now to take advantage of the current opportunities presenting themselves.

"We are all faced with a series of great opportunities brilliantly disguised as impossible situations."

Charles R Swindoll

"Learn everything you can, anytime you can, from anyone you can - there will always come a time when you will be grateful you did."

Sarah Caldwell

You will be in one of three positions right now. Either you have an offline business you want to bring online to enhance your services or expand your market. Alternatively you may have a business idea which you believe will make a great web based service offering. Finally you may already have an on-line business and be looking for ways in which to increase your web site traffic, sales conversions or product and service offerings.

Whichever situation you currently find yourself in, you will be able to benefit by the tools and techniques of Niche Internet Marketing. Read through this entire book twice. Make sure you take notes throughout the entire book. I highly recommend you write all over the pages with your own notes, highlighting sections that are of more importance to you. I also suggest you get some post it notes so you can keep a track of all the pages and sections in the course.

This book also has a full contents listing and is fully indexed so you can search by topic. Additionally there is a glossary of terms which you can reference if you are unsure of the definition of any term to do with the internet or internet marketing.

Also make sure you download my free Internet Marketing Toolbar at www.WebsiteMarketingToolbar.com. The Internet Marketing Toolbar contains links to all the tools and resources you will require to market your website successfully on the internet. It also has links to all the top search engines which you can search directly from the toolbar. As a bonus when you download and install the Internet Marketing Toolbar, your site will be added to the Internet Marketing Toolbar Traffic Generation system which will help generate extra traffic to your site, by rotating your link at all other member sites, as well as creating quality incoming links to your site.

Also be sure to visit and sign up for free to be a member of my Website Marketing Forum at: http://www.NicheInternetMarketing/forum. Here you will find a community of like-minded individuals who you can discuss all your Internet Marketing needs with, share ideas, find joint venture partners, or announce your new product releases.

The main thing to remember is to get started straight away. Do not delay. Every day is another opportunity which you must seize a hold of and make the most of. Now that you have all the tools, resources and knowledge at your fingertips, there is nothing in the way of you and Niche Internet Marketing success. So get to it, get started right now. Use the information contained here in to become the ultimate Niche Internet Marketer! Carpe Diem! Seize the day!

Chapter 4

Motivation, Focus and Persistence –
The importance of staying motivated, maintaining laser-like focus and being persistent in your quest for internet success.

Motivation is a fire from within. If someone else tries to light that fire under you, chances are it will burn very briefly.
Stephen R. Covey

Water continually dropping will wear hard rocks hollow.
Plutarch

To achieve anything worthwhile in life, you must ensure you have the tenacity and drive to be able to stay focused long enough to achieve your goals. But how do you maintain this motivation? For a start you need to set some clearly defined short, medium and long term goals for your internet business. Write them down and make sure you display them somewhere prominent.

Your goals should be clearly defined and concise. Make sure your goals are achievable and set them in order of increasing difficulty. Your Internet Marketing goals should be directly related to the areas you need to work on to improve your overall site performance.

I highly recommend you join a newsletter or newsgroup relating to the topic of Internet Marketing. I have a free Internet Marketing Newsletter at www. WebsiteMarketingMagazine.com. You can sign up free and keep abreast of all the latest developments in the Internet Marketing world. Joining an Internet Marketing Newsgroup or discussion group will enable you to exchange ideas and techniques with fellow Website Marketers. In addition you will be able to ask questions of your fellow discussion group members when you get stuck.

Keeping up to date with the world of Internet Marketing will give you some fuel to motivate your own success. Another excellent idea is to study success stories of those who have already become a success with their own internet business. There are several sources of success stories on the net. The longer you stay involved in the Internet Marketing game, the more successful sites and business owners you will get to know. Here is a great source of successful website owners:

http://www.secretstotheirsuccess.com
Another great place that Internet Marketers gather is
http://www.WarriorForum.com

When you find a successful site, it is a great idea to deconstruct what they have done to become so successful. See how they have put their site together, and exactly what elements their site is made up of. What have they done differently? Are they listed high in the search engines? Did they have a big advertising budget, both on and offline? Is it a new service or product? Is their product or service available elsewhere? Do the website owners have a business background? Or is this their first foray into the world of running a business?

Let other web sites be your inspiration. Learn from others and mirror their success.

Another great motivational website (Not Internet Marketing specific) is: http://www.motivateus.com
Check it out, I use this every day to give my brain the positive input to stay focused and driven towards my goals! You should use it too.

Action item! >>>

> Go to http://www.motivateus.com

> Bookmark the site

> Read through some motivational quotes to get you inspired and in the right frame of mind.

> Go to http://www.secretstotheirsuccess.com/

> Read through some success stories for ideas and motivation. Study, study, study!

Chapter 5

Finding your Niche

> "The essence of life is finding something you really love
> and then making the daily experience worthwhile."
> Denis Waitley

Jim was a full-time office worker. He worked conscientiously from 9am to 5pm and made good money for his employer. It had been this way for years. The problem was that Jim felt he wasn't living his passion, or following his true destiny. Somewhere along the line, Jim had just accepted the cards that fate had dealt him. Rather than quit his job and start again, Jim started a small we business selling memory cards for cameras, as this was closely related to photography – Jim's true passion.

Before making any investment in time or money developing an idea that might be stillborn, Jim browsed all the technology and business news sites to check trends in memory card sales, and to ensure the market for his product would remain buoyant in the years to come. All Jim's research came back positive so he decided to proceed with his idea. Jim also did a search at Overture and found that 27,000 searches per month were performed for the term 'memory card'. If Jim added all the child keyphrases such as 'sony memory card', there were well in excess of over 100,000 searches performed per month, and this was just on Overture! If Jim extrapolated this out, conservatively with the big search engines Jim could be looking at a market with over 250,000 searches per month. Jim knew he had the demand, now he just needed to formalise a strategy to target the niches within that market.

Jim started off small, did some research and invested in a domain name at www.GoDaddy.com, and a monthly hosting account which was about $16 in the first month, and $6 monthly thereafter for the hosting. Jim registered www.JimsMemoryCards.com

Jim set up his website to be search engine optimised, with a lot of relevant keywords in the sales copy of the homepage. Jim used www.NicheBot.com and the Overture search term suggestion tool to ensure he had a good spread of keywords, and that they were relevant and actively being searched on a monthly basis. Jim came up with the following top 20 keywords he would target:

- sd memory card
- xd memory card
- memory card reader
- ps2 memory card
- cheap memory card
- memory cards
- psp memory card
- memory stick
- micro sd memory card
- memory stick pro duo
- memory stick duo
- memory stick micro
- 1gb memory card
- usb memory stick
- camera memory card
- memory stick pro
- memory sticks
- 1gb sd memory card
- sd memory cards
- 2gb memory card

Jim had his niches!

Before adding any product to his website, Jim set up a forum that he was able to automatically install for free as part of his hosting package at GoDaddy. In the forum Jim created a number of key categories relating to types of memory cards, brands of memory cards and other related keywords. Jim then Googled 'free articles' and browsed all the article sites on the web to find articles relating to memory cards. Jim published these articles in the relevant categories in his forum. Jim also created a signature file for his profile in the forum that linked back to www.JimsMemoryCards.com.

Being a passionate amateur photographer, Jim had built up quite a bit of knowledge about photography and photography equipment over the years – including memory cards. So Jim decided to write a few articles of his own. Over about a week, Jim wrote 5 articles about different types of memory cards, each article was about 300 words long. Jim then went back to the article sites that he had searched for articles in previously and submitted his articles. Each of his articles had a link back to www.JimsMemoryCards.com.

At this point just to be sure his site was added to the major search engines, Jim went to msn.com and google.com and submitted his website manually.

As this was Jim's first foray into marketing online, he wanted to test the water firstly before he committed to any full-blown investments. Instead of purchasing his own inventory, Jim did a search on the internet for companies that had affiliate programs for memory cards. Jim found a company (http://www.memorysuppliers.com) that paid 12% commission for every sale and handled all the backend payment processing and fulfilment of product. This is just what Jim was looking for, so he signed up on the spot. Once signed up, Jim logged into his account and cut and paste the html code supplied by his affiliate program into the home page of www.JimsMemoryCards.com. The html code supplied by the affiliate program is dynamic, and automatically displays the latest products and pricing, so Jim won't need to worry about updating the code when prices change, old products are discontinued or new products come out. All Jim needs to do is promote his website and collect his commission every month.

Jim's site was going well. He was receiving a commission check for a little over $500 every month – which wasn't bad considering Jim only spent a few hours a week updating and maintaining the site. It was easy for Jim to stay motivated and spend a few hours on his site every night, as this was his passion and was making him a nice little nest egg on the side that he could spend on his family or spoil himself.

Every week Jim wrote a few more articles and submitted them to different article sites. Jim made sure that his articles included many of his niche keywords he had researched earlier. Jim had been doing a bit of reading up on Internet Marketing and knew that if he could increase his number if incoming links to his site he could increase his rank in the search engines for whatever his anchor text in those links was. Jim knew he wanted his anchor text to be 'Memory cards'.

Jim did a bit of research, and found some free software to create a link directory on his own website (http://linkmachine.net/). Jim installed the software and started adding links to his directory. Jim the drafted an email that he sent to potential link partners explaining that he had linked to their site, and inviting them to link to his site. Jim sent this email out to 20-30 potential link partners a week. Of those about 10 partners per week started to link back to www.Jims-MemoryCards.com. Over the next few months Jim noticed these extra incoming links having a positive effect on his ranking within the search engines, and subsequently his commission payouts had increased to $750 per month.

Jim was getting a lot of emails from customers of his site. Although Jim loved interacting with his customers, it was starting to become a burden and eat into his time with his family. Jim collated a list of all the typical types of questions he would receive, and standard responses to each. Jim set up an FAQ (frequently asked questions) page and published all his questions and answers. Jim also decided to install a free forum software that was included as part of his hosting package at GoDaddy. This was visitors to his site could interact with each other and ask each other questions rather than directing them to Jim. The FAQ and forum worked quite well, and cut Jim's emails by 85% per week.

Up until now, Jim's traffic to his website had been organic. In other words, Jim had not paid for any advertising for his site, all the traffic was generated by organic searches within the search engines, and the incoming links from Jim's link partners and articles he had published. Jim felt he could make more sales, and decided to invest a portion of the money he was making each month into advertising with Google Adwords. Jim logged onto Google Adwords and created an account. Using his previously researched list of keywords, Jim created an ad campaign and created 4 Adwords ads so he could test the effectiveness of each.

SD Memory Card	cheap memory card
The cheapest memory on the net	The biggest variety on the net
Sign up now for your free account!	Visit us for all your memory needs!
www.JimsMemoryCards.com	www.JimsMemoryCards.com
Memory cards	2gb memory card
Biggest variety, cheapest prices	Other sizes also, cheapest prices
Visit our forum to view feedback!	Visit to see our huge range!
www.JimsMemoryCards.com	www.JimsMemoryCards.com

Jim set his daily budget to $10 which would keep the monthly advertising costs under $300. After a month, with advertising of just under $300, Jim had increased his commission check to $1500 for the month. So for $300 in advertising, Jim had generated an additional $750 of income, or $450 extra profit.

Jim noticed that his top performing
Google Adwords ad was:

With a click through ratio (CTR) of 8.7%. So Jim paused his other 3 ads, and directed his entire advertising budget to this ad. The next month, Jim noticed that his commission check was still around the $1500 mark. Although Jim had directed his full advertising budget to his best performing Google ad, as he was only paying for the clicks he received, he would only ever receive a finite amount of traffic for his money.

Over the next couple of months, Jim slowly increased his advertising budget on Google AdWords. This in turn had an impact on his commission check at the end of the month. Jim also set up a newsletter that visitors to his site could subscribe to and is building an email list that he sends a monthly newsletter to with news about memory cards, and any special offers he is running for the month.

After about 12 months, Jim had achieved a very good monthly income from his website, but he recognised the limitations of being an affiliate for somebody else's products – his profit would always be set at 12%.

As Jim now had a legion of repeat happy customers, and subscribers to his email list, he decided to investigate companies that sold memory card products wholesale. As Jim didn't want to set up handling and shipping facilities at his home office, the wholesaler had to offer dropshipping services also. Jim found a wholesaler with a good reputation, and after doing some calculations figured out that he could purchase inventory and make 66% profit rather than 12% he had made for the previous 12 months as an affiliate.

To make the transition from affiliate to retailer, Jim decided to test the water by ordering his most popular product from the wholesaler initially, and offering it for sale along side his catalogue of affiliate products. As his product would effectively be competing with that particular product in his affiliate catalogue, Jim decided to offer his at a 10% discount, still earning him a 56% profit – 44% above what he was earning for that product as an affiliate.

Jim set up a sales page for his new product on his website, setup a free shopping cart software on his website (linked to his paypal account) and placed a small initial order with his wholesaler.

Over the next month, Jim's profits jumped $200 – after introducing only one product of his own. The wholesaler took care of all the dropshipping, so there was no additional work for Jim other than setting up the product sales page and links on the home page of his site, then placing the order with his wholesaler. The wholesaler holds the stock for Jim, and ships the orders as they are sent through automatically from Jim's ordering software. All Jim needs to do is run a report every month to see how much stock he needs to re-order, and check his Paypal balance.

There was a bit of work involved in setting up his own products for sale, but Jim sees the potential. Jim plans to add more of his own popular products for sale over the coming months, and slowly phase out his affiliate program for all but the less popular products that Jim will not be stocking. Jim's business is currently producing an income of $1700 part-time, however with his new product lines being introduced over the coming months, Jim has forecast a minimum of $5000 profit monthly within the next 6 months. Jim then plans to negotiate a 4 day work week with his current employer so he can devote the 5th day to starting another web business that he can put on auto-pilot.

Action item! >>>

> Grab a piece of paper and jot down a brief outline of your action plan.

> Consider what niches you will target, how many hours per day or evening you can devote to your website, how much money you can set aside to invest in your domain name, hosting and any advertising you would like to do.

> What is your target monthly income?

> What is your ultimate goal? Do you wish to free up time to travel more? Do you want the satisfaction of running your own business? Do you want to spend more time with your family?

Chapter 6

Finding Products and services to sell

"Know where to find the information and how to use it - That's the secret of success."

Albert Einstein

Like Jim from www.JimsMemoryCards.com, you don't initially need a product or service to sell. You can sell other people's products and services and earn a commission. In fact this should be your strategy, allowing you to focus on building a quality website with a decent amount of traffic to begin converting visitors into sales. Let your chosen affiliate program fulfil all the orders and payment processing initially.

So where can I find products and services to sell?

Here is a list of the more popular affiliate sites on the internet:

Commission Junction www.cj.com

ClickBank - http://www.clickbank.com

You will find many products listed here under many different categories that you can sell for a slice of the profit.

Something to keep in mind is that as you gain experience and build a successful website, you may become a provider of an affiliate program at these sites and have a network of affiliates selling your products for you!

But let's not get ahead of ourselves just yet. You can join these sites as an affiliate and search amongst all the categories for products you wish to sell that fit in with the theme of your site.

For example, Jim logs into his Commission Junction account, clicks on the 'Get Links' tab and does a search for 'memory cards'. He is presented with a list of 16 advertisers that he can apply to become an affiliate for by ticking the checkbox next to the advertiser name and selecting 'Apply to program'. A list of the suppliers for 'memory cards' is shown below:

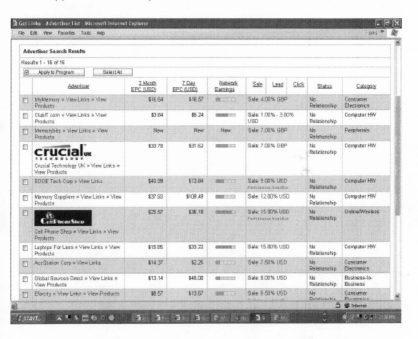

The amount or % you can earn per sale is listed, and you can click on the advertiser name to find more about the company or website.

Similarly, with www.ClickBank.com, you can go to the marketplace (http://www.clickbank.com/marketplace.htm) and search for products to sell. However be aware that ClickBank mainly sells informational products such as e-books and products that can be delivered electronically such as software.

The other way to search for affiliate programs is to got Google.com and type in the type of affiliate program you are looking for. In Jim's case, he would search for 'memory card affiliate program'. This will return all the independent affiliate programs that are not associated with any of the larger affiliate networks.

Of course if you are a keen writer with some skills or experience that you think may be saleable, go ahead and create your own e-book. You can then create a website, and an account at ClickBank.com and start marketing your own informational product and keeping 100% of the profits.

If you want to earn more than just affiliate commissions, then go to Google and do a search for 'wholesale' and / or 'dropshipping' for your chosen niche. For example Jim would do a search for 'memory card wholesale' to find companies where he can purchase his product wholesale. You may also wish to do a search for 'Manufacturer' or 'producer' and go straight to the source, however normally you may only be able to purchase in mass quantities if dealing directly with the manufacturer.

Do a search on Ebay for your chosen niche product. This will give you a good indication of the type of competition you will be up against, and they types of prices product is selling for. You will also be bale to gauge the demand of product depending on the numbers of bids on auctions, and items sold for 'Buy it now' sales.

Action item! >>>

> Create a free affiliate account at the following 2 sites:

> Commission Junction www.cj.com

> ClickBank - http://www.clickbank.com

> Log in and search for products in your chosen niche

> Got www.Ebay.com and search for products in your chosen niche. If you can't find any, then you may have found an untapped market ready to be fulfilled!

> Go to www.Google.com and conduct a search for your niche keyword paired with the following keywords: wholesale, dropship, manufacturer, producer.

> E.g. 'memory card wholesale'

Page Structure –
How you should structure your pages. What tags, meta data and elements to include on your page for maximum spiderability.

"The important thing is not to stop questioning. Curiosity has its own reason for existing. One cannot help but be in awe when he contemplates the mysteries of eternity, of life, of the marvellous structure of reality. It is enough if one tries merely to comprehend a little of this mystery every day. Never lose a holy curiosity."

Albert Einstein

There is some consternation as to what constitutes the perfectly structured page, what elements to include to increase your search engine rankings, and the amount of keyword density required in your text to keep the search spiders happy and coming back for more.

I have tried and tested every conceivable combination and permutation of html elements and content in my pursuit of the perfectly optimised html page. (For the overall site structure, and linking strategies, please see later chapters.) In this chapter we will concentrate on the structure of the html page itself and what I believe to currently be the best configuration for an optimised page, and therefore higher rankings in the search engines.

The debate about keywords rages on. In my opinion, the search engines do use them, but not to the degree they used to. I have been privy to some research whereby the testers created dummy pages with obscure keywords.

The keywords themselves were not included anywhere within the content of the web page, title, subtitles or alt text. These pages were then submitted to Google. Once spidered, the pages appeared for searches on the obscure keyword, thus debunking the myth that Google does not use keywords. However, the case will probably be that your web pages will contain keywords which are not obscure, and you will be optimising for these highly competitive keywords. So you will need to rely on a variety of methods and techniques other than the primitive use of keywords. In conclusion, my advice at this stage is to use them, as it cannot hurt. I have seen no evidence of Google or any other search engine demoting sites for the use of keywords, unless used incorrectly. (see later chapter on keywords.)

Keyword density
Please see the later chapter entitled 'Keyword density'.

Placement of menu
Some conventional wisdom would suggest that as search engine spiders crawl your HTML from the top down, having your menu at the top of the page will inhibit your search engine rankings. Some marketers will even go so far as to position their menu on the right hand side of the web site. From my experience, I have seen well ranked pages with menus in all positions, so I think for the most part you should not be too worried about where you position your menu. However, using static html links for your menu from your main page may produce PR bleed, so it may be a wise decision to construct the menu on your main page using dynamic links. Please see the later chapter entitled 'Dynamic verses Static links' to find out how.

Newsletter lists
For details of how to build an opt-in email list, please see the later chapter entitled 'Building and maintaining a high quality opt-in email list that you can sell to again, again and again.'

Blogs
For more information on Blogs, please see the later chapter entitled "The Niche Blog Mininet".

Email Links
If you want to include your email address on your page so people can get in touch with you, be sure to use an email submit form. This way, programs

which are designed to scour the net to find email addresses embedded into html will not pick up your email address. Another simple way to avoid this is to use a simple script like the one below:

```
<script language="Javascript">
<!--
var name = "YOURNAME"
var domain = "YOURDOMAIN.COM"
document.write("<a href='mailto:" + name + "@" + domain + "'>")
document.write(name + "@" + domain)
document.write("</a>")
//-->
</script>
```

Case Study >>>

> http://www.Magazine-Template.com is a great example of how a page and site should be structured. The website contains one key product – a magazine template, and is generating on average $360 per day with no maintenance.

> The website contains a forum, a mini e-course / newsletter list and multiple keywords.

Action item! >>>

> Go to http://www.Magazine-Template.com

> View all the elements that go into making this a successful web page.

Note: the product is in a very tight niche market, the sales letter focuses on selling only one product, examples of the product are shown, a testimonial is included. Visitors can sign up to a 10 lesson mini ecourse which gives 10 more opportunities to stay fresh in the mind of the customer and potentially sell them the product down the line.

Chapter 8

Site Structure –
How you should structure your entire site to ensure that the search engines will search your entire site, and spider everything they see for the keywords you are targeting.

"Marketing is not an event, but a process . . . It has a beginning, a middle, but never an end, for it is a process. You improve it, perfect it, change it, even pause it. But you never stop it completely. "
Jay Conrad Levinson

Your internal linking structure is very important. You will need to ensure that you target your page rank to your home page, or sales page whichever is appropriate. There are a number of ways in which you can do this, some of which I will describe below.

Basically you need to have as many pages in your site linking back to your home page as possible. The way that you do this is you have one external link from your home page to an index page. From your index or contents page, you have 2 way links to all of your other pages. From all your other pages you have a one way link back to your home page. All the links should be text based and descriptive including the keyword you are trying to target in the search engines. It is also beneficial to include an articles page and links page. The articles page would be linked to from your index page, and list links to a variety of articles on your related topic. Here is a list of sites you can get articles for free to reprint:

Ezine Articles.com http://www.ezinearticles.com
GoArticles http://www.goarticles.com
Web Pro News http://www.webpronews.com
Site Reference http://site-reference.com
AD http://www.articledashboard.com
Free Articles http://www.topica.com/lists/free_articles
Articles Base Directory http://www.articlesbase.com
Articles.Web.Com http://www.articles.web.com
Gobala Krishnan http://articles.easywordpress.com
DirectoryGold Article Directory http://articles.directorygold.com
Afro Articles - Article Marketing Directory http://www.afroarticles.com/article-dashboard/
InfoWizards Free Content Articles http://content.infowizards.com
Article Friendly http://www.articlefriendly.com
Article Submission http://www.articlewheel.com/
Top-Affiliate.com http://www.top-affiliate.com/articles
Free Articles for Reprint http://www.articles-hub.com
Article Ardvaark http://nero.byethost15.com
Submit Your New Article http://www.submityournewarticle.com
ArticleRich.com http://www.articlerich.com
ArticleCafe.net http://www.articlecafe.net
Your Free SAtellite http://www.your-free-satellite.com/index-2.html
The Add Articles Directory http://www.add-articles.com
Article Blotter http://www.articleblotter.com
1Article World http://www.1articleworld.com
ABC Article Directory http://www.abcarticledirectory.com/
eArticlesOnline.com http://www.earticlesonline.com
Weight Loss Buddy Articles http://www.weightlossbuddy.com
dk-article http://www.article.com
ArticleSnatch - The Best Place to Grab Articles http://www.articlesnatch.com
Talkin Mince Article Directory http://www.talkinmince.com
Just Articles http://www.JustArticles.com/
Article-Buzz - Free Article Directory http://www.article-buzz.com/
Free Ezine Articles Site http://freezinesite.com
Tips Tricks Resource Portal http://www.tips.com.my
Altrana http://www.altrana.com

I Need Content http://finance.groups.yahoo.com/gro...Need_Content
Gather Success http://www.gathersuccess.com/articles/
The Article Trunk http://www.ArticleTrunk.com
Ezine Finder http://www.ezinefinder.com
ArticleCircle - Free Articles Directory http://www.articlecircle.com
JPServicez Search Articles, Tutorials, Journals and How Tos Directory http://www.jpservicez-searcharticles.com
ArticleStreet.com http://www.articlestreet.com
Traffichelp4u Article Dashboard http://www.traffichelp4u.com
Online MLM http://www.onlinemlm.com/articledirectory/
Good Info Home http://goodinfohome.com
Article Blender Directory http://www.articleblender.com
Isins Article Directory http://www.isins.com/articles/
The Articleshelf http://www.articleshelf.com
IntPedia Articles http://articles.intpedia.com
Articles2K http://www.articles2k.com/

Your links page will be linked to from your index page, and include a variety of tightly themed link pages of sites you have exchanged links with. The preceding internal linking structure has been thoroughly tested by many Website Marketers and is highly successful. The diagram below demonstrates the optimal internal linking structure for a site:

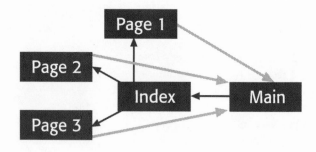

The above configuration allows PR from the web pages within your site to be concentrated to the main page of your site.

When first designing my internal linking structure, I found the following resources invaluable in learning exactly how to do it:

- Michael Campbell's Revenge of the Mininet
  http://leighburke.dmrev.hop.clickbank.net/

- Derek Gehl's Internet Marketing Course
  http://www.marketingtips.com/t.cgi/646322/

- Leslie Rohde's Dynamic Linking Ebook, which comes free with Michael Campbell's 'Revenge of the mininet'.

Case Study >>>

> http://www.Accommodation-Thailand.com is a great example of how to structure a site for an affiliate product or program. The website sells accommodation in Thailand, and is generating on average $120 in affiliate revenues per day with no maintenance.

> The website contains an articles database with relevant content articles that link back to the homepage. This increases the homepage PageRank.

Action item! >>>

> Go to http://www.Accommodation-Thailand.com

> On the homepage note the YouTube video that has been inserted to give the website visitor a taste of Thailand.

> Click on 'Thailand Articles and discussion' at the bottom of the page.

> Note the relevant articles themed into different Thailand destination categories.

Chapter 9

MiniNet Structure –
How to structure a series of Mini sites to focus page ranking on your main site to increase search engine rankings. A very powerful technique.

"It's not what's happening to you now or what has happened in your past that determines who you become. Rather, it's your decisions about what to focus on, what things mean to you, and what you're going to do about them that will determine your ultimate destiny. "

Anthony Robbins

There is powerful evidence that suggests building a variety of mini sites and linking them all together, channelling page rank to one particular web page within the whole structure will boost that sites rankings within the search engines considerably.

Using the mini site strategy, you sacrifice page rank from a variety of websites within your mini net, to boost the rankings of you main or sales page. Each of the main websites within your mini net structure should be a fully-fledged website in its own right. This means that you will need to register separate domain names for each website within your mini net. As far as hosting goes, there is no evidence to suggest that having multiple domain names hosted on the same IP address, whether static or dynamic will cause the search engines to penalise that group of websites or mini net. But if you have cheap access to a number of hosting accounts, it can't hurt to have your different sites hosted on different IP addresses. Search engine algorithms are always changing, so better safe than sorry!

Where you WILL run into trouble is if you start repeating content across the mini net. You need to make sure that the content for all the different websites within the mini net is unique and not repetitious. Although, you definitely want a recurring theme throughout your mini net, try to focus each website within the mini net on a different set of related keywords or theme.

Each website within the mini net should be constructed as described in the "Site Structure" chapter of this course. This way you will ensure that PR is funnelled to the main page within each website. Additionally, you should include a link from each main page of each website within the mini net, pointing to the main page of your main site within the mini net. The diagram below demonstrates this technique:

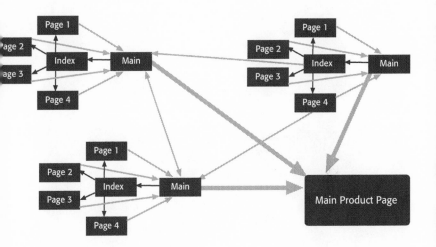

As you can see from the above diagram, a mininet is created by the bi-directional links represented by the orange lines and arrows. PR within each site is concentrated from all the pages within the site back to the Main page for each respective site. This concentrated PR is then passed from the main page of each site within the mininet to the main sales page for the mininet. This is a very powerful and effective technique.

I learnt all about Mini nets by reading Michael Campbell's Revenge of the Mininet. Get your copy by clicking the link below. Michael explains how and why this concept is here to stay. Included are heaps of diagrams detailing different linking methods. Michael also includes a free copy of Leslie Rodhe's Dynamic Linking Ebook, which explains all about PR and directing maximum PR to your main product page.

Check out Michael Campbell's Revenge of the Mininet:
http://www.RevengeOfTheMininet.com

Case Study >>>

> http://www.isidore-of-seville.com/petra/ is a great example of how to structure a series of sites to create a mininet structure. Tim Spalding has created a series of interlinked websites about fascinating historical subjects such as Cleopatra, Machu Picchu, Alexander the Great and Hieroglyphs.

> Tim has monetised his sites by including Adsense ads to other relevant content on the right of his pages.

Action item! >>>

> Go to Google.com and type in 'Petra'. You'll notice that http://www.isidore-of-seville.com/petra is listed about 9th (which isn't bad for a history buff with 5 websites!)

> Scroll to the bottom of the page, and notice the other web pages in the network.

> Click on 'Machu Picchu on the web', scroll to the bottom of the page and you will notice the list of links to other sites in the network.

> Browse around the network of sites, and notice how they are keyword rich, and contain many interlinked pages within each site and within the network of sites itself.

Chapter 10

Site content and themes –
How to focus your content to create a strong theme throughout your pages, site and mininet.

"Welcome every morning with a smile. Look on the new day as another special gift from your Creator, another golden opportunity to complete what you were unable to finish yesterday. Be a self-starter. Let your first hour set the theme of success and positive action that is certain to echo through your entire day. Today will never happen again. Don't waste it with a false start or no start at all. You were not born to fail."

Og Mandingo

All web sites should contain a theme that is tightly bound towards one keyword, keyphrase or a series of related key words. All incoming links to your web site should come from sites that have a similar theme. You need to choose 2-3 primary keywords, and additionally you will need to have 3-5 secondary keywords or keyphrases. A great way to look for related keywords and keyphrases is to use one, or a combination of the services below:

- **Overture Search Term Suggestion Tool:**
  http://inventory.overture.com/d/searchinventory/suggestion/
  Overture is a very basic keyword generation tool. But the best thing for beginners is it is absolutely free to use. Type in a keyword and press enter, and Overture will query its database and return the keyword with a value. The value indicates how many searches are being conducted for that keyword or keyphrase per month on Overture. To get a rough idea of how many searches are being conducted for the same keyword on Yahoo, MSN and Google, times this figure by a factor of 5.

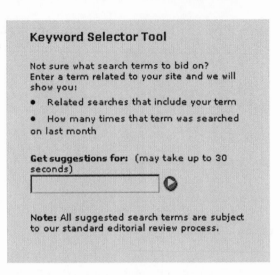

Keyword Selector Tool

Not sure what search terms to bid on?
Enter a term related to your site and we will
show you:

- Related searches that include your term

- How many times that term was searched
on last month

Get suggestions for: (may take up to 30
seconds)

Note: All suggested search terms are subject
to our standard editorial review process.

In addition to your initial keyword query, the Overture database will return
a list of related keyphrases. Although these results are limited to keyphrases
containing the keyword you initially searched for. You can click on any of these
keyphrases to make the search more granular yet again.

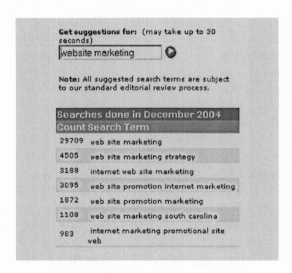

Get suggestions for: (may take up to 30
seconds)

website marketing

Note: All suggested search terms are subject
to our standard editorial review process.

Searches done in December 2004	
Count	Search Term
29709	web site marketing
4505	web site marketing strategy
3188	internet web site marketing
3095	web site promotion internet marketing
1872	web site promotion marketing
1108	web site marketing south carolina
983	internet marketing promotional site web

I would suggest if you want to make your keyword analysis using Overture more thorough, run your initial keyword through a thesaurus (an online thesaurus can be found here: http://thesaurus.reference.com/) That way you will be able to perform multiple manual searches on synonyms of your original keyword.

- **Wordtracker:**
  Wortracker compiles a database of terms that people search for. You enter some keywords, and Wordtracker tells you how often people search for them, they also tells you how many competing sites use those keywords.

  Wordtracker helps you find all keyword combinations that bear any relation to your business, service or product - many of which you might never have considered.

  You'll find out how popular these keywords really are.

  Then for each major search engine, directory, and pay-per-click service Wordtracker will show you how many other sites will be competing with you.

  To find out more, http://www.Wordtracker.com

- **Google Adwords keyphrase selector tool:**

  https://adwords.google.co.uk/select/
  https://adwords.google.com/select/

Once you have created a Google Adwords account, you can log in and start creating your campaigns. Once you have created an ad, you can insert your own keywords, or type an initial keyword into the grey box, and click the 'Get more keywords' button:

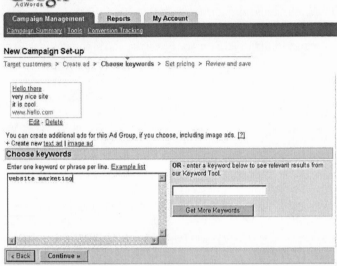

When you click the get more keywords button, Google Adwords will come back with a list of the most popular keywords as show below:

Google Adwords will also return a list of similar keywords like the ones below:

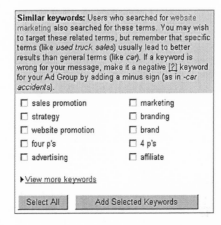

So using this tool, it is now possible to create highly targeted Adword campaigns, but also use this research when creating content and themes for your websites.

- Nichebot: http://www.NicheBOT.com

Nichebot is another great free resource. Below are details and descriptions of all the site's features.

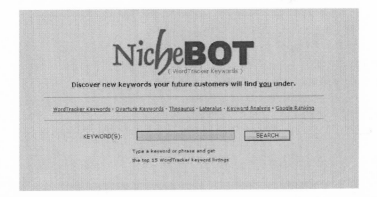

What is the "WordTracker Keywords" tool?

NicheBOT's WordTracker Keywords tool provides a limited aspect of the Wordtracker keyword service together with Google results which reveals active keyword phrases that people use to search. Enter a search term, and Niche-BOT will return 15 variations of that search term, which people have used to search the search engines. This tool is useful for developing lists of keywords for the search engines, and finding new and/or in-demand niches and keyword phrases.

What is the "Overture Keywords" tool?

NicheBOT's Overture Keywords tool incorporates Overture's keyword suggestion tool and Google to reveal active keyword phrases that people use to search. Enter a search term, and NicheBOT will return 100 variations of that search term, of which people have used to search the search engines in the *prior 30 days*. This tool is useful for developing lists of keywords for the search engines, and finding new and/or in-demand niches and keyword phrases.

What is NicheBOT's "Thesaurus?"

NicheBOT's Thesaurus tool, provided by aspects of Wordtracker, reveals synonyms of, and related keywords to your search term. This tool is useful for finding new keywords/phrases that might not be so obvious.

What is NicheBOT's "Lateralus?"

NicheBOT's Lateralus tool, provided by aspects of Wordtracker, reveals related keywords/phrases that people often associate with your search term. This tool is useful for finding keywords/phrases that might not be so obvious.

What is NicheBOT's "Keyword Analysis?"

NicheBOT's Keyword Analysis, provided by aspects of Google, reveals key ranking factors in Google for your search term. This tool is useful for analyzing your keyword competition in Google.com.

What is NicheBOT's "Google Ranking?"

NicheBOT's Google Ranking Tool, provided by aspects of Google, allows you to locate the position of any Web-site in Google, for an unlimited number of keywords and phrases. This tool is useful for quickly finding the ranking of your Web-site(s).

Action item! >>>

> Go to http://www.isidore-of-seville.com/petra

> Click on 'Overviews and gateways' on the left menu

> Note the content listed, and links to other relevant Petra content.

> Click on the other menu items in the left menu and note the tightly themed Petra content on each page.

> This is what we call a theme. The site and network of sites target tightly related themes, and are not generalist in nature.

Chapter 11

Hosing and IP address considerations –
free, paid, static or dynamic?

"Vow to be valiant; Resolve to be radiant; Determine to be dynamic;
Strive to be sincere; Aspire to be attuned."
William Arthur Ward

You should ALWAYS have your own domain name for a website with the nameservers set up to point to your own hosting account. What this actually means is that you will need to edit your Domain Name account and update the nameserver information with the nameservers given to you by your hosting company. You will then need to go into your online hosting administration account, and set up an account for your new domain, so when the nameservers for your domain are updated and propagate across the internet, the 2 settings will be able to synchronise with each other and start working. The normal timeframe for this propagation to take place is 24 hours, but often times happens within hours.

Here are the steps you should take to set yourself up.

- Get yourself a hosting account. Try my hosting service, I got fed up with hosting companies, so started my own!: www.GuerillaHosting.com. Here's the standard list of features for every hosting account. And you have the added advantage that I, or one of my staff can take you step by step through the setup process:
- Guerilla Hosting Standard features:

Every one of our servers offers the latest stable versions of top programs. From ASP and ASP.NET to PHP to MySQL and Perl anything you ultimately want to develop on your website you can do with us. Besides just providing some of the fastest servers on the internet (as rated by independent Alexa/Amazon.com) we offer as STANDARD on all of our plans the following features (free of charge of course).

Secure Operating Systems Used:
Linux, FreeBSD, Windows 2003

E-Mail Accounts Available:
No Limit*

MS SQL Database Limits:
Unlimited*

MySQL Database Limits:
Unlimited*

Commonly Used Features Available:
Webmail (NeoMail, horde, Squirrelmail)
E-Mail Redirect (Forwarders)
E-Mail Autoresponders
E-Mail Mailing Lists
Custom Error Pages
Unlimited FTP Accounts

Graphical Site Statistics Programs:

AWStats

Webalizer
Analog
Raw Log Access
Error Log Access

Programming Languages Available:
Perl (version 5.8+)
PHP (version 4.3.4+)
MySQL (version 4.0.18)
phpMyAdmin (version 2.5.6)
Tomcat (available on some servers)
ASP (on Windows Servers)
ASP.NET (on Windows Servers)

Shopping Carts (Free & One Click Install):

Interchange
Agora

Forums & Content Software (Free & One Click Install):
InvisionBoard (Forum Software)
phpBB (Forum Software)

One Click Installation of the following CGI Scripts:
Counter
Guestbook
Clock
Random HTML
& More

**And of Course each domain account has its own cPanel
control panel separate from all others.**

Network, Data Center & Servers

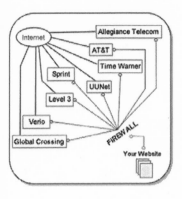

Network:

To ensure maximum redundancy and uptime we use multiple providers. Our current internet providers are as follows:

Allegiance Telecom -- **1 Gbps** (GigE)
Global Crossing -- **1 Gbps** (GigE)
Level 3 -- **1 Gbps** (GigE)
Sprint -- **1 Gbps** (GigE)
Time Warner -- **1 Gbps** (GigE)
UUNet -- **1 Gbps** (GigE)
Verio -- **1 Gbps** (GigE)
AT&T -- **DS3**

Data Center:

When you host your sites with us you can rest assured that the server you are on is being monitored 24 hours a day with onsite staff. So if you have a problem at any hour of the day someone is available to solve any problems or respond to any requests.

Server Specs:

One of most commonly asked questions is what are the specifications of the server my site will be on. The servers we purchase are state of the art, top of the line, servers from Dell Corporation. Each has, on average, has two Intel Xeon Processors, 2 GB of ECC RAM, and SCSI hard drives configured in RAID for redundancy. We spend thousands of dollars on our servers for quality servers. We don't believe servers are the place to save money because our clients demand reliability not cost cutting.

- When you sign up for your hosting account, the hosting company should provide you with 3 addresses.
- The first address will normally be at a secure Http site, and have the format Https://www.YourHostingProvider.com/YourName. It could also be in the form of an IP address such as Https://156.128.128.1/cpanel In the preceding example, cPanel is the account administration module you will use to administer your account. The cPanel account administration panel is shown below:

CPanel allows you to administer your server remotely. Don't worry, it's not that complicated, and you will only use a few very handy features of your cPanel.

- The second and third addresses your hosting provider will supply you with are your nameservers. These are the addresses you will have to update in the information for your specific domain name to point them to your host so everything will synchronise and work. Nameservers usually take on the format ns1.YourHostingProvider.com and ns2. YourHostingProvider.com write these down or print them out and keep them somewhere safe.
- Register your domain name. I highly recommend www.GoDaddy.com, I use them all the time now.
- Make sure you remember your username and password for your domain name account. Write them down, or print off your confirmation and keep them somewhere safe.
- Go into your domain name administration panel. If for example you registered your domain name with www.GoDaddy.com , goto the homepage for GoDaddy, and enter your customer login name and password and click Login.

- You will be presented with the following account administration screen:

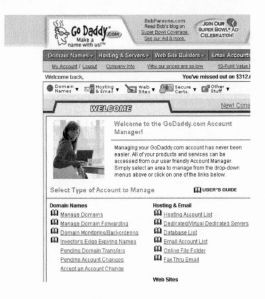

- Click on 'Manage Domains'
- Click on the domain name you want to modify the nameservers for.

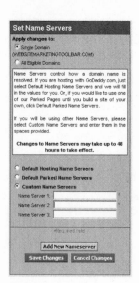

- Choose Custom Name Servers, then fill in your name server information in the 'Name Server 1' and 'Name Server 2' fields.
- Click Save Changes.
- You should allow 24 hours after making name changes for the changes to propagate across the internet. Although often it happens quite faster than this estimated time, often within hours!

Action item! >>>

> Go to http://www.GoDaddy.com

> Bookmark the site

> Do a search for a domain name and familiarise yourself with the process and other services offered.

> If you haven't already done so, register your domain name!

Chapter 12

Domain name considerations – .com. .net. .org or other, should keywords be included, what about hyphens?

"If you hack the Vatican server,
have you tampered in God's domain?"

Aaron Allston

You should always buy a new domain name for each new website that you launch. Domain names are so cheap these days, that the cost is negligible. Not only does a unique domain name help you to build brand recognition, but it looks more professional, and allows you to have different domain names to submit to the search engines, keeping each site a unique entity on its own, and tightly themed.

I strongly recommend that if you have a project in process, you purchase the domain name sooner rather than later. This way your domain name will have a history by the time you go to use it. Even if you just put a temporary site up with a few pages based on the topic the site will eventually be about, this will give you a distinct advantage with the search engines in the future when you go to your launch phase. Additionally, you don't want to get logos created only to find that somebody else has registered the domain name in the meantime no matter how unique you think it is.

If you can, always choose a .com or your country specific domain ie. *.co. uk, *.com.au, *.co.nz, *.ca. Unless you are a charitable organisation, you don't need a .org, and it just looks second rate and unprofessional. Despite rumours, there are still an abundance of .com domain names available as they expire and people don't re-register them.

Deleted domain names can be purchased here: http://www.deleteddo-mains.com. But it is not entirely necessary to fork out for a deleted domain name. Depending on your industry and your niche market, with a bit of research, and imagination, you should be able to come up with a catchy, memorable name within a few hours.

The best company I have found to register my domain names through is www.GoDaddy.com. The reason I like to use GoDaddy, is they offer some of the cheapest prices around (I own over 150 domain names, so I like to keep prices as low as possible! Plus not getting ripped off is one of the creed's of the Internet Marketing Guerilla!) But in addition to just the price consideration, GoDaddy allows you to manage your domains completely by yourself with a convenient online control panel. Some registration companies charge extra for them to do simple changes that you could have done yourself quite easily if they had given you the permissions in the first place! These are called full-service companies, they are a rip-off, and not needed, steer clear of them. www.GoDaddy.com do offer a whole heap of additional add on services which will cost you extra, but I never go for these, as I find for the most part, they are just bells and whistles I do not require. If you are concerned about privacy, you may wish to go for the domain locking option, which will allow you to have a privately registered domain, so your details will not be viewable to the general public via conducting a WhoIS search. Conducting a www.WhoIS.net lookup will ordinarily enable you to find out who a domain name is registered to, when the domain name was registered and expires, as well as the email addresses of the administrative and technical contacts. If the domain name is private, this information will not be viewable. Another way to achieve the same result is to register the domain name under a company or business name.

www.BuyDomains.com are quite good too, and offer a similar range of features, but are more expensive than GoDaddy per domain name.

I have also used www.DotEasy.com as they used to offer free web hosting with their domains, and still do. But I have found that as other companies lowered their prices for registering domains, www.DotEasy.com has stayed almost static, no doubt to absorb the cost of the free hosting offered with the domain. If you don't have any domain names at all, and will require hosting as well, this is a good all in one option.

The good domain name registrars offer you domain name generation tools. With these, you can enter a keyword, or a series of keywords, and the domain name generation tool will come back with a variety of domain name options with these keywords, as well as synonyms of these keywords included in the domain name. An example taken from www.GoDaddy.com is the list below for the keyword "websitemarketing":

WEBSITEMARKETINGONLINE.COM
WEBSITEMARKETINGWEB.COM
WEBSITEMARKETINGHOME.COM
WEBSITEMARKETINGPAGE.COM
1STWEBSITEMARKETING
1WEBSITEMARKETING
4WEBSITEMARKETING
ACTIONWEBSITEMARKETING
ACTIVEWEBSITEMARKETING
ADULTWEBSITEMARKETING
ADVANCEDWEBSITEMARKETING
AFFILIATEWEBSITEMARKETING
AFFORDABLEWEBSITEMARKETING
AWESOMEWEBSITEMARKETING

BANANAWEBSITEMARKETING
BCWEBSITEMARKETING
BETTERWEBSITEMARKETING
BUSINESSWEBSITEMARKETING
CANADAWEBSITEMARKETING
CANADIANWEBSITEMARKETING
CHICAGOWEBSITEMARKETING
CHRISTIANWEBSITEMARKETING
CORPORATEWEBSITEMARKETING
CREATIVEWEBSITEMARKETING
CURRENTWEBSITEMARKETING
DOMAINNAMESFORWEBSITEMARKETING
EASYWEBSITEMARKETING
ECOMMERCEWEBSITEMARKETING
EWEBSITEMARKETING

The domain name generator will also tell you whether the .net, .com and .org versions of the domain name are available. If the domain name is available, you simply click on the link to register the domain name on the spot.

There is some evidence that suggests including keywords in your domain name separated by hyphens will enhance your search engine positioning. If you do choose this approach, do not go overboard, and limit your keywords to 3. Do not use any post or suffix hyphens, and never use 2 hyphens in a row. For example, these would be bad domain name choices: www.-Website-Marketing. com, www.Website--Marketing.com . You should still try to make an effort to give your domain name some kind of brand recognition. Make your domain name easy to remember. Something catchy which rolls off the tongue.

Remember domain names are not case sensitive, so if you registered www. mydomain.com for example, you could advertise it to your customers as www. MyDomain.com and it would still direct them to the same site.

Action item! >>>

> Go to http://www.GoDaddy.com

> Do a search for the domain name 'Niche'.

> Scroll down and see the domain name suggestions

> You will note 'Premium Domain Names' and 'Additional Domain Names.'

> Under Additional Domain Names click 'See other domains like this.'

> Choose some options under 'Smart Search' and click 'Search'

> If you don't already have a domain name, and are starting to crystallise what niche you are going to target, do some research at GoDaddy now. If you find a short, snappy, memorable name that you like, purchase it now! Carpe Diem! (Seize the day)

Chapter 13

Building a shopping cart, how databases & dynamic content will affect your rankings.

> "Whoever said money can't buy happiness simply didn't know where to go shopping."
>
> Bo Derek

If you sell or intend to sell products or services from your web site, you may already use, or will eventually require a shopping cart facility and payment system. There are a variety of payment methods available on the net, but the features you should look for are reliability, not too costly to implement or run (ongoing costs), ease of use for your customers, and above all security. You will also require the ability to list multiple products at varying price points.

There are a variety of free shopping cart software available for free on the internet, here are some of the better ones:

http://www.online-store.co.uk/

http://www.securenetshop.com/

http://www.agoracart.com/

An even better solution would be to set up your hosting with a company that includes free shopping cart software that can easily be installed on your server via an automatic script, and then tweaked with a minimal amount of configuration. www.GuerillaHosting offer free shopping cart scripts, that can be automatically installed from your cPanel.

Of course another option is to use https://www.paypal.com. Paypal has a number of handy built in tools for merchants. They handle all the security, and deal with all checks and credit cards. The only thing the merchant has to do is pay a small fee on every transaction. Payment buttons can be encrypted to increase security, and once successful payment is received, the customer can be redirected to a thank-you page, or a product download page. Some of the Paypal Merchant tools are shown below:

Additionally, the Paypal code you add to the HTML of your web pages can be edited to include additional code for running affiliate programs. Paypal is by far the most popular payment method on the internet today.

Another option if you are selling digital products (music, video, e-books) is to use a service such as http://www.clickbank.com

Services such as Clickbank will fulfil all your orders for you for a small fee. Additionally they have a large network of affiliate marketers that you can plug into and utilise to sell your product or service. This will save you a lot of the legwork in finding affiliates to promote your product or service. Many of the top internet marketers use this service to sell their products.

Action item! >>>

> Go to http://www.PayPal.com

> Click on the 'Products and services' tab.

> Browse the available services and familiarise yourself.

> If you don't already have a Paypal account, sign up for one now.

> Paypal is safe, secure and universally recognised as a payment system on the internet.

Chapter 14

Building and maintaining a high quality opt-in email list that you can sell to again, again and again.

"The Internet is clearly about more than sports scores and email now. It's a place where we can conduct our democracy and get very large amounts of data to very large numbers of people."

Frank James

Building an opt-in email list is a great way to be able to reach your customers again and again for little or no cost, and minimal effort. In recent years, this marketing method has become less effective due to the advent of spam filters and blockers. But as new technology becomes available to help get authorised messages through, we should see the amount of blocked genuine messages dropping. There are many advantages of selling to your existing customers. You are a known name to them. They have already bought from you before, so know they can trust you, and will be highly motivated to buy from you again.

There are many products on the market to help you build your own opt-in email list. They are generally database driven and offer a variety of features that will help you build and manage your list. Some of the products are quite expensive, so you might want to try a free product first, or a managed service. I recommend that you have your own hosted service though. That way you will be in total control of your list always.

Many hosting services offer a variety of free plug-in tools that will allow you to automatically install your own free email list builder onto your server. The hosting service I own and use, www.GuerillaHosting.com, offers this service along with other plug-in tools which will be of invaluable use to you when using Niche Internet Marketing tactics on the net. The email list management tool I use is called PHP list and is shown in the screenshot above.

The hosting management interface is called cPanel and allows you to fully manage your site online with no other need for special software or tools, as cPanel is entirely web based. Many hosting companies offer this, so find the best service and deal that you can!

Once you have your email list management tool installed, it is just a matter of promoting your service to your website visitors. One of the best ways I found to do this is to use a popunder window from your home page. The popunder window will load when your main page loads. It will remain unseen until the user closes the main window, at which time it will become visible, and hopefully entice your visitors to sign-up. You should also be aware that the large majority of internet users have a pop-up blocker installed on their system these days. So don't rely solely on a pop-up window to promote your email list service. You should also include links on your regular HTML pages. Another good service is http://www.InstantAttention.com/ which allows you to create eye-catching java-based pop-ups which remain in the main browser window, and therefore are not blocked by regular pop-up blockers. Check it out.

I always offer an incentive to my potential email list members to encourage them to sign up. A free gift of some sort can be offered, which people will receive once they sign up. This free gift could be a free piece of software, free articles about whatever product or service you offer, or the chance to win some sort of other prize in a monthly draw. If you sell an ebook, you could offer members who sign up to your email list the opportunity to receive the first 2 chapters free. This is a win/win situation, as your potential customer gets to try your ebook, and you get the possibility of having a new customer if they liked the first 2 chapters, and bought the whole ebook to read it all.

See how I promote my free newsletter service at :
http://www.NicheInternetMarketing.com

If your free gifts are the type that can be delivered electronically, then have them all on a web page on your site so members who sign up for your email list can easily download them automatically after sign-up. Make sure there are no other links to your free downloads page from anywhere else within your site. Additionally, you will need to ensure that your free downloads page is included in your robots.txt file so the search engines don't list your free downloads page in the search engines. Alternatively, include a robots entry in the metadata for this page. Here is an example of what you should include if you don't want the page indexed by the search engines:
<META NAME="ROBOTS" CONTENT="NONE">

When new members sign up to your email list, they will automatically receive an email asking them to confirm their sign up to your list. To do this they will need to click on a link within the email. They may also need to additionally enter a code or their email address when they are directed to your mail list confirmation page. Here is an example of what this email should look like:

From	: Leigh Burke <noreply@websitemarketingnewsletter.com>
Reply-To	: noreply@websitemarketingnewsletter.com
Sent	: Friday, 17 December 2008 5:13:27 PM
To	: new_subscriber@email.com
Subject	: Please confirm subscription to Leigh Burke's Niche Internet Marketing Newsletter

Almost welcome to Leigh Burke's Niche Internet Marketing
Newsletter...

Someone, hopefully you, has subscribed your email address to Leigh Burke's
Internet Marketing Newsletter at http://www.NicheInternetMarketing.com

If this is correct, please click this URL to confirm your subscription:

http://www.NicheInternetMarketing.com/lists/
?p=confirm&uid=128cc06b158d2acabcab7a06cec7

Once you confirm your subscription, you will receive a confirmation email
which contains the link to your FREE e-book "The Robots are Here", as well as
your 18 page BONUS report by internet marketing expert Corey Rudl.

If this is not correct, you do not need to do anything, simply delete this message.

Kindest Regards,

Leigh Burke

www.NicheInternetMarketing.com

(This is called double opt-in) Once they have successfully signed up to your mail list, they will receive another email confirming their sign up. This email will also include the link to your free downloads page. This ensures that only people who have successfully signed up will receive your free downloads. This final confirmation email will also include unsubscribe details for when members want to unsubscribe from your list. Below is an example of how you should set this email out:

From   : Leigh Burke <noreply@NicheInternetMarketing.com>
Reply-To : noreply@NicheInternetMarketing.com
Sent   : Friday, 17 December 2008 5:13:48 PM
To   : new_subscriber@email.com
Subject : Welcome to Leigh Burke's Niche Internet Marketing News-
letter!

Welcome to Leigh Burke's Niche Internet Marketing Newsletter!
Please keep this email for later reference.

Your email address has been added to the following mailinglist:

*Leigh Burke\'s Niche Internet Marketing Newsletter

To unsubscribe please go to:

http://www.NicheInternetMarketing.com/lists/
?p=unsubscribe&uid=128cc06b1cvfed2ac3989c89ab7a06cec7

and follow the steps.

To update your details and preferences please go to:

http://www.NicheInternetMarketing.com/lists/
?p=preferences&uid=128cc0623423d2ac3989c89ab7a06cec7.

To download your FREE "The Robots Are Here" Ebook, please go to:

http://www.NicheInternetMarketing.com/freebook/RobotsHere.pdf

To get your BONUS 18 page report by Internet Marketing Expert Corey
Rudl, please go here:

http://www.marketingtips.com/t.cgi/646322/

Kindest Regards,

Leigh Burke
www.NicheInternetMarketing.com

Make sure you keep in contact with your list on a regular basis. This will ensure that they remain responsive to your communications. Include your name and email list details in the subject line of any email communications you send to your list. This will ensure that maximum readership is obtained. You need to build a familiarity with your readership, so you offer them value for their time taken to read your newsletters and other promotions. This way, you build up a bond of trust between yourself and your list. Be sure to have a link on every email that gives members of your list the opportunity to unsubscribe.

Include your name or product name at the start of the subject, as this will be seen first, and a longer subject line may get cut off. For example:

Leigh Burke's Niche Internet Marketing newsletter – June edition

OR

Niche Internet Marketing Newsletter – June edition

In the above examples, 'June edition' may get cut off, but 'Leigh Burke' and 'Niche' will always be seen, so my subscribers will immediately know the email is from me, or relating to my Niche products. Another point to note is the 'From' email address you use should have your name or product name before the '@', as most email software takes this first half of an email address and uses it in the from field when displaying email to the recipient. For example:

Leigh_Burke@NicheInternetMarketing.com

Niche_Marketing@NicheInternetMarketing.com

Newsletter@NicheInternetMarketing.com

In the above examples the 3 emails would appear to be from 'Leigh_Burke', 'Niche_Marketing' and 'Newsletter' respectively. Now although it IS a newsletter you are sending, it is likely that the recipient receives a number of newsletters along with a whole heap of SPAM. So you will want to make sure you use a 'From' email address that distinguishes you from the crowd. Of the above 3 email addresses, the ones beginning with 'Leigh_burke' and 'Niche_Marketing' would be the best to use as they are more descriptive than just 'Newsletter'.

Additionally you may want to send 2 versions of every email that you send to your list. The first version will be a full text version. Containing all the content of your emailing, including links and subject matter. The next version you send will simply be an email explaining if they missed your first emailing, they can find the newsletter at your website via a link you will include in this email. The link will connect them to a HTML version of your newsletter stored on your website. This also has the other advantage of providing extra high quality, themed content for your website. Here is an example of the second version of the email you should send:

From	: Leigh Burke <noreply@NicheInternetMarketing.com>
Reply-To	: noreply@NicheInternetMarketing.com
Sent	: Friday, 17 December 2008 5:13:48 PM
To	: new_subscriber@email.com
Subject	: Leigh Burke's Niche Internet Marketing Newsletter December edition now available!

Friday 17 December 2008

Dear subscriber,

In case the email filters ate your newsletter, this is a just
quick note to let you know the latest Niche Internet Marketing
Newsletter is now available online. You can read it here:

Print Version: http://www.NicheInternetMarketing.com/new.pdf

Online Version: http://www.NicheInternetMarketing.com/new.html

In this issue:

1) The art of blogging.
2) Taming the beast that is Google.
3) Is podcasting the way of the future?
4) The hottest products in Santa's sack this Christmas.
5) Make a mint on Ebay.

And many more useful hints, tips and articles, enjoy!

If you have already received the newsletter by email, please disregard
this reminder and thank you for reading.

Leigh Burke
http://www.NicheInternetMarketing.com

The reason for this second email is that you will need to be aware that a lot of automatic spam filters these days filter emails with words they think may identify them as spam email. This is done automatically by a process known as Bayesian filtering. Bayesian filtering is the process of using Bayesian statistical methods to classify documents into categories. As your initial email contains your full newsletter, and therefore more words, there is a higher probability that it may be identified as spam by the spam filters.

Bayesian filtering gained attention when it was described in the paper A Plan for Spam by Paul Graham, and has become a popular mechanism to distinguish illegitimate spam email from legitimate "ham" email. Many modern mail programs such as Mozilla Thunderbird implement Bayesian spam filtering. Server-side email filters, such as SpamAssassin and ASSP, make use of Bayesian spam filtering techniques, and the functionality is sometimes embedded within mail server software itself.

Bayesian email filters take advantage of Bayes' theorem. Bayes' theorem, in the context of spam, says that the probability that an email is spam, given that it has certain words in it, is equal to the probability of finding those certain words in spam email, times the probability that any email is spam, divided by the probability of finding those words in any email:

$$P(spam|words)spam = \frac{P(words|spam)P(spam)}{P(words)}$$

A great free email list manager is PHP list. This can be loaded automatically for free if you have your hosting at www.GuerillaHosting.com.

Another great free list manager is Infinite responder available at http://infinite.ibasics.biz/. Infinite responder allows you to build a list quickly and easily. Infinite responder also allows you to set up a series of auto-responder messages to be sent at intervals automatically. This is a great way to set up a free mini e-course like the one found at http://www.Accommodation-Thailand.com

Action item! >>>

> Go to http://www.NicheInternetMarketing.com

> Click on the 'Newsletter' tab

> Sign up for my free newsletter

> Note the confirmation emails you will receive, and the pages you are automatically redirected to

> Go to http://infinite.ibasics.biz/ and download this free software to your Niche Internet Marketing directory on your local drive.

Chapter 15

What is PR and how do you increase yours? The importance of PR for your site.

"When soldiers have been baptized in the fire of a battle-field, they have all one rank in my eyes."

Frank James

Rank 6

PR stands for page rank and was invented by Google. Pagerank is a value from 0 to 10. Pages which are newly crawled by googlebot (googlebot is the spider which constantly crawls the net for Google looking for and indexing new pages.) , will have a Pagerank of 0. The more popular a site becomes, which is calculated by the amount of incoming links, as well as other factors, the higher the Pagerank for that site/page becomes.

When you exchange links with other sites, they will put a link from their site to yours, and you will reciprocate by placing a link from your website to theirs. That incoming link they give you, will slightly increase the Pagerank for your site. In addition Google will take into account the quality and volume of the content on your site.

PR takes time to build up. Once Google has crawled your site, allow at least 3-6 months to build up your PR. Generally websites with a higher PR will be ranked higher in Google and other search engines.

When considering whom you will exchange links with, generally if you have sites linking back to your site with a higher PR, it will be more beneficial to the overall ranking of your own site. But having said that, the more sites you have linking back to your site the better off you will be, regardless of the PR of the links.

PR is a constantly debated topic. There are many theories about how to boost your PR, but in general these are just theories, and Google's algorithm is a tightly guarded secret. The best we can do as Niche Internet Marketers is to ensure we do everything possible to boost our PR within Google, without doing anything to become banned by the googlebot. See the later chapter about what not to do to get banned by Google.

Action item! >>>

> Go to http://toolbar.google.com

> Download the Google Toolbar if you don't already have it installed

> Once Installed, select 'Settings', 'Options'

> Click the 'More' tab, and select 'Page rank and page info', click OK, Click OK again to confirm.

> Now browse to any page on the internet, and you will notice the PageRank displayed on the Google toolbar.

Chapter 16

Incoming Links –
How many should you aim for?
Does the quality matter?
Should they be high PR?

"It is a mistake to look too far ahead.
Only one link of the chain of destiny can be handled at a time."
Winston Churchill

Generally the volume of incoming links matters more greatly than the quality of all the incoming links. Generally you should aim for a mix of high PR incoming links as well as the volume of your incoming links themselves. That is to say you should not accept an incoming link just because they don't have a high PR. In general you should ensure that the sites that link to you have the same kind of theme as yours.

There is a great tool for finding link partners and building up your incoming links. You are able to manage emails to your potential incoming link partners, as well as building your own links database. Additionally, the incoming links they do find for your site are based on a series of keywords that you build up within the software itself. That way you ensure that all incoming links adhere to the tightly specified theme that you create.

The tool is Zeus the internet Marketing Robot. You can download a free trial copy and give it a go. Check it out here: http://www.cyber-robotics.com

When I was learning about building up my incoming links, I found Glenn Canady's Gorilla Internet Marketing course invaluable. Glenn wasn't by any means the pioneer of building incoming links, but he took what he learnt and turned it into an art form. He has dominated the search engines and in particular Google for high popularity keywords for over 18 months now. His techniques are fresh, but evolving, and most importantly, they work! Check out his ebook here: www.GlennCanady.com

The more high quality links you have linking back to your sales page, the higher the PR for your sales page will become, and the higher your rankings in the search engines will become. The following diagram shows how incoming PR is calculated:

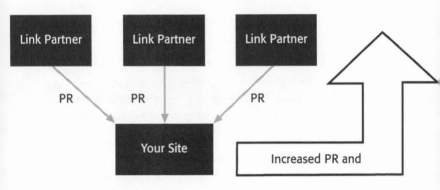

Chapter 17

Outgoing Links – PR bleed, should this be avoided?

"If you prick us, do we not bleed? if you tickle us, do we not laugh?
if you poison us, do we not die? and if you wrong us, shall we not
revenge? If we are like you in the rest, we will resemble you in that"
William Shakespeare

PR bleed is when you have too many outgoing links from your main, home
or products page. To avoid this, you should structure your site such that any
outgoing links to other pages occur from a page that is linked to from your
main product page. You may also like to include a dynamic link menu, so that
the search engine spiders will not regard your menu as outgoing links from
your main page, and thus will not penalise PR.

For further information on dynamic linking, see the chapters on 'Page
Structure', 'Site Structure', and 'Dynamic verses Static links.'

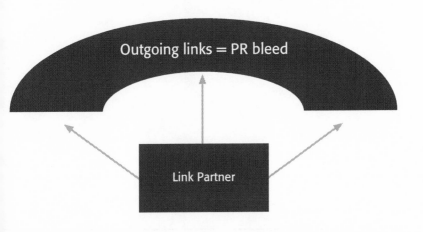

Action item! >>>

> Go to http://www.linkdirectory.com/

> Observe how a link directory is structured and works

> Click 'Submit Link' at the top, and observe the options available to submit a link.

Chapter 18

Dynamic verses Static links –
What is a dynamic link? How can you use these to increase PR and rankings?

"The universe is dynamic. When we are creative, we are the most alive and in touch with it."

Brad Dourif

A static link is a standard html text link like this:

<a href=http://www.examplelink.com>Goto Example Link</a>

This can be used to link to pages internally in your website, or externally to other websites. The disadvantage of a static html link is that the search engine spiders will always follow them. So if for instance you were trying to funnel all the PR (PageRank) from your site and other sites linking to your site to your homepage, it would be a disadvantage to have other links from your homepage, as these would allow PR to be lost from your homepage. This is called PR bleed.

The advantage of a dynamic link is that it looks and functions exactly like a normal text link, however dynamic links will not be followed by the search engine spiders. Therefore you are able to create links from your main or homepage to other areas in your site or to external websites without losing PR for your homepage. The following is an example of the code you would need to include on your homepage to create dynamic links:

```
<a href="javascript:window.location='your-domain-here' "> Your link text here </a>
```

Then to get the status bar to show your target URL, rather than the whole javascript string, you can create a mouseover effect with the following code:

```
<a href="javascript:window.location='your-domain-here' "
onmouseover="window.status='your-domain-here' "
onmouseout="window.status=' '"> Your link text here </a>
```

If you want to learn all the advanced methods for creating a site with dynamic links, then I highly recommend Michael Campbell's 'Revenge of the Mininet:

http://www.RevengeOfTheMininet.com

Chapter 19

L ink Sharing –
How to get link partners. What to say. Tools and processes for managing your links.

"Society cannot share a common communication system
so long as it is split into warring factions."
Bertolt Brecht

As mentioned previously by far the best tool for finding and maintaining link partnerships is:

Zeus the internet Marketing Robot. You can download a free trial copy and give it a go. Check it out here: http://www.cyber-robotics.com

Remember Glenn Canady is really the current king of building incoming links to boost search engine rankings. Check out his successes and ebook here: www.GlennCanady.com

The tools above will take out the majority of the leg work for you when trying to find link partners and maintain your links page. But here are my top tips for building targeted incoming links.

Ensure that you only accept or offer links to and form link partners who have a website with a theme which tightly matches your theme. Don't worry if they are a competitor, customers are going to find them anyway. It will be beneficial for you both to set up a reciprocal link agreement.

Make sure you also have a 'Link To Us' section on your website for visitors who want to set up a link with you manually. This page should allow them to submit their link to you via a form, and have the code they can cut and paste into their own links page for your link. Always ensure that your link partners link back to your home or main product page, via a descriptive text link that contains the keywords you are optimising for. A banner or graphic link although it may look more attractive will actually funnel less PR to your home page.

You can include a link code generator on your Link To Us page, an example of one can be found here: http://www.javafile.com/websitetool/linkgen/linkgen.php

You must be extremely careful when sending out email to potential link partners, as any un-requested email could be considered spam. If the potential link partner already runs a linking program on their site, they should be quite open to the offer of a link partnership. If you are accused of sending unsolicited email, simply send a polite reply explaining that you were merely requesting a joint venture, and leave it at that.

To further ensure you are not accused of sending spam, always make sure your link requests are professional, personalised, and for links back to a professional looking site that sell actual products or services.

Here is an example letter you can use when sending an email to potential link partners:

```
=========================================================

Greetings [website owner],
I am the CEO and President of MyCompany, a company
that provides flugelbinders. I have developed a web
site on flugelbinders that has lots of top quality
content on topic x and topic y.
I like your site on [topic] at [url] and I would like
to exchange links with your site, http://www.your-
site.com.
This will benefit us mutually by increasing both our
indirect traffic from higher search engine and direct
traffic from the links. If you'd like to swap links,
please do email me back and I'll add your link to my
resources page at http://www.mycompany.com/resourc-
es/ within 24 hours. If you could include the loca-
```

tion of my link that would be appreciated.
If you'd like to include a description, please use
the following
(describe your site in 15 words or less)
Feel free to include a description for your link as
well. I very much look forward to hearing from you.
As a special thank-you for linking to my website,
I'll send you a copy of my 20 page report 'Excellent
Internet Marketing Report'.
Warm Regards,
Your Name
President
YourCompany
http://www.yourcompany.com
(area code) Phone-number
P.S.: If you'd like to use a graphic I can send one.
I'd be glad to add one next to your link as well.
Thanks again!

==

In the above email, note that I have included the offer of a free report as
an incentive to linking to my website. This is a nice token gesture, and will increase the chances of potential link partners linking to your site. Remember to
be accurate, concise and extremely polite stating exactly what your aims are.

Make sure that you link to the potential partner before sending any email
at all.

Action item! >>>

> If you have a website, Google 10 potential web sites that
you could link with who have related content and a link
program

Chapter 20

Getting listed in the Search Engines –
How to submit your site to the major search engines. Yahoo, Google, MSN.

"To act with common sense according to the moment, is the best
wisdom I know; and the best philosophy is to do one's duties,
take the world as it comes, submit respectfully to one's lot;
bless the goodness that has given us so much happiness with it,"

Horace Walpole

To submit your site to Google, go to the following URL:
http://www.google.com/addurl/?continue=/addurl

You will need to enter the URL of your site, including the http://www. The comments field is not really needed as it does not affect anything. Make sure you also enter the squiggly coloured letters, so Google can distinguish that this is a human rather than automated submission. Finally, click "Add URL".

To submit your site to MSN, go here:
http://search.msn.com/docs/submit.aspx?FORM=WSDD2

Add your URL to Google

Share your place on the net with us.

We add and update new sites to our index each time we crawl the web, and we invite you to submit your URL here. We do not add all submitted URLs to our index, and we cannot make any predictions or guarantees about when or if they will appear.

Please enter your full URL, including the http:// prefix. For example: http://www.google.com/. You may also add comments or keywords that describe the content of your page. These are used only for our information and do not affect how your page is indexed or used by Google.

Please note: Only the top-level page from a host is necessary; you do not need to submit each individual page. Our crawler, Googlebot, will be able to find the rest. Google updates its index on a regular basis, so updated or outdated link submissions are not necessary. Dead links will 'fade out' of our index on our next crawl when we update our entire index.

URL:

Comments:

Optional: To help us distinguish between sites submitted by individuals and those automatically entered by software robots, please type the squiggly letters shown here into the box below.

riess

Add URL

Enter the characters displayed in graphical format, then enter your URL, including the http://www. Finally click "Submit URL".

You can suggest a site to Yahoo, but you will need to sign up free as a Yahoo member first. Once you have signed up, go here:

http://submit.search.yahoo.com/free/request

Type in your URL and click on "Submit URL".

Action item! >>>

> Go to http://www.google.com/addurl/?continue=/addurl

> Add a URL to the Google index

> If you don't have a web page to add, add somebody else's to see how it works

Chapter 21

Getting listed in the Directories –
How to submit your site to the major directories. Yahoo, DMOZ.

"Every day I get up and look through the Forbes list of the richest people in America. If I'm not there, I go to work."

Robert Orben

Suggesting your site to the DMOZ open directory project can be worthwhile.

The Open Directory Project is the largest, most comprehensive human-edited directory of the Web. It is constructed and maintained by a vast, global community of volunteer editors.

For full instructions on suggesting your site to DMOZ, go here: http://dmoz.org/add.html

I don't recommend spending too much time or effort on trying to get listed with DMOZ though. Getting an un-established site listed with DMOZ can be notoriously difficult and time-consuming. Your time may well be better spent concentrating on getting listed with Google, MSN and Yahoo as shown in the previous 'Getting listed in the search engines' chapter.

Action item! >>>

> Go to http://dmoz.org

> Browse categories that your website could be listed in

> Observe how you can suggest a site to DMOZ

Chapter 22

Keyword Selection –
How to select keywords, key terms (or phrases) for your site.

"Publishers are in a very keyword-rich environment. Because publishers sell words, not products, they need to delve into the large set of keywords they already have and use the words or phrases that their buyers do to search the Web. By developing programs based on how your audience searches, publisher's search engine marketing programs will thrive."

Pamela Springer

The 2 best and free keyword selection utilities are:

> The Overture Keyword Selector tool -
> http://inventory.overture.com/d/searchinventory/suggestion

> And

> Nichebot – http://www.nichebot.com

- Overture Search Term Suggestion Tool: http://inventory.overture.com/ d/searchinventory/suggestion/
  Overture is a very basic keyword generation tool. But the best thing for beginners is it is absolutely free to use. Type in a keyword and press enter, and Overture will query its database and return the keyword with a value. The value indicates how many searches are being conducted for that keyword or keyphrase per month on Overture. To get a rough idea of how many searches are being conducted for the same keyword on Yahoo, MSN and Google, times this figure by a factor of 5.

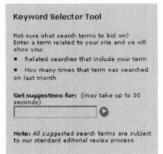

Keyword Selector Tool

Not sure what search terms to bid on? Enter a term related to your site and we will show you:
- Related searches that include your term
- How many times that term was searched on last month

Get suggestions for: (may take up to 30 seconds)

Note: All suggested search terms are subject to our standard editorial review process.

In addition to your initial keyword query, the Overture database will return a list of related keyphrases. Although these results are limited to key phrases containing the keyword you initially searched for. You can click on any of these keyphrases to make the search more granular yet again.

I would suggest if you want to make your keyword analysis using Overture more thorough, run your initial keyword through a thesaurus (an online thesaurus can be found here: http://thesaurus.reference.com/) That way you will be able to perform multiple manual searches on synonyms of your original keyword.

A full breakdown of the features of www.NicheBot.com can be found in the previous chapter 'Site content and themes '.

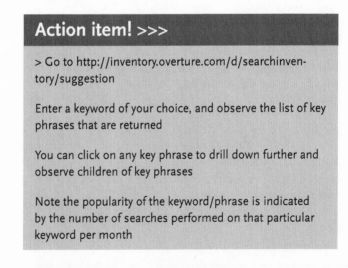

Action item! >>>

> Go to http://inventory.overture.com/d/searchinventory/suggestion

Enter a keyword of your choice, and observe the list of key phrases that are returned

You can click on any key phrase to drill down further and observe children of key phrases

Note the popularity of the keyword/phrase is indicated by the number of searches performed on that particular keyword per month

Keyword Density – How your selected keywords should be used within your site structure.

"There is something else which has the power to awaken us to the truth. It is the works of writers of genius. They give us, in the guise of fiction, something equivalent to the actual density of the real, that density which life offers us every day but which we are unable to grasp because we are amusing ourselves with lies."

Simone Weil

The recommended density is 3-7%. This means that your keyword(s) should repeat 3-7 times for every 100 words.

Sound easy? Imagine having 10 keywords and trying to repeat each one 3-7 times per 100 words of text -- it's practically impossible. Instead, pick two or three of your most important keywords and try to use them 3-7 times for every 100 words.

Bear in mind that this is only a rough guide, and all your web pages should be different to ensure they have a natural feel to them rather than a machine generated HTML page, or one following the strict guidance of a template.

Chapter 24

Getting to the top of the Search Engines for your targeted keywords –
How to get your site high rankings for your targeted keywords.

"We think too small, like the frog at the bottom of the well.
He thinks the sky is only as big as the top of the well. If he surfaced,
he would have an entirely different view."

Mao Tse-Tung

Getting your website to the top of the search engines for your chosen keyword is not an impossible task, but it will take time, patience and knowledge. You need to use everything you have learned in this e-book. More importantly, you will need to keep on learning new techniques, refining your knowledge, and testing new methods for yourself.

Here is a brief recap of what you will need to do:

- Register your domain as early as possible so it will have time to age for the search engines. Try and include keywords in your domain.
- Setup your hosting account, and point your DNS information for your domain to your hosts DNS server.

- Register a number of domains and host them on different IP ranges.
- Set up blogs on all your websites, and funnel PR from all the sites in your mininet to your main sales page. Include high quality, relevant themed content in all your blogs and mininet sites.
- Follow all the rules for building a tightly themed site, using the keyword tools described in this e-book.
- Submit your main site to MSN and yahoo. If you have another website that is already indexed, better still, put a link from that website, and wait for the search engines to find your site, and mininet and naturally spider them.
- Continually and gradually update the quality content of your blogs with fresh new articles and content.
- Seek out quality link partners, and always get them to link back directly to your main sales page via a text link with your chosen keywords embedded.

Chapter 25

What to avoid so the search engines don't ban you.

"Books won't stay banned. They won't burn. Ideas won't go to jail."
Alfred Whitney Griswold

Google lists the following specific guidelines about what practices to specifically avoid so you don't get banned by the search engines:

Quality Guidelines - Basic principles:

- Make pages for users, not for search engines. Do not deceive your users or present different content to search engines than you display to users, which is commonly referred to as "cloaking."
- Avoid tricks intended to improve search engine rankings. A good rule of thumb is whether you would feel comfortable explaining what you have done to a website that competes with you. Another useful test is to ask, "Does this help my users? Would I do this if search engines didn't exist?"
- Do not participate in link schemes designed to increase your site's ranking or PageRank. In particular, avoid links to web spammers or "bad neighborhoods" on the web, as your own ranking may be affected adversely by those links.
- Do not use unauthorised computer programs to submit pages, check rankings, etc. Such programs consume computing resources and violate our Terms of Service. Google does not recommend the use of products such as WebPosition Gold™ that send automatic or programmatic queries to Google.

Quality Guidelines - Specific recommendations:

- Avoid hidden text or hidden links.
- Do not employ cloaking or sneaky redirects.
- Do not send automated queries to Google.
- Do not load pages with irrelevant words.
- Do not create multiple pages, subdomains, or domains with substantially duplicate content.
- Avoid "doorway" pages created just for search engines, or other "cookie cutter" approaches such as affiliate programs with little or no original content.

These quality guidelines cover the most common forms of deceptive or manipulative behaviour, but Google may respond negatively to other misleading practices not listed here (e.g. tricking users by registering misspellings of well-known websites). It is not safe to assume that just because a specific deceptive technique is not included on this page, Google approves of it. Webmasters who spend their energies upholding the spirit of the basic principles listed above will provide a much better user experience and subsequently enjoy better ranking than those who spend their time looking for loopholes they can exploit

Chapter 26

The Niche Blog Mininet

> "The man is a success who has lived well, laughed often, and loved
> much; who has gained the respect of intelligent men and the love
> of children; who has filled his niche and accomplished his task;
> who leaves the world better than he found it, whether"
>
> Bessie Stanley

I have devised an absolutely brand new technique that works fantastic wonders when trying to increase your search engine rankings! This method is a combination of a couple of other methods that are already know in the internet marketing community, but have never been used together to produce such outstanding results.

If you aren't exactly sure what a blog is, then go here to see an example: http://www.websitemarketingcourse.com
I bought this domain to help promote Niche Internet Marketing. But the approach I have taken is rather than create a traditional site with advertising copy and fancy pictures, I would create a site that consisted of purely a blog with high quality content. Now once the search engine spiders picked up on this, and started ranking the site higher up in the index, then I could tweak the site to display the content I wanted – pointing web surfers back to my sales pages.

A mininet is a collection of websites, all with different domains. There is a main website, and supporting websites that channel PR back to the main website sales page.

Now imagine the power of the mininet combined with the index and crawlability of a high quality blog site, and what you get is nothing short of amazing. Essentially what you end up is a network of tightly themed blog sites, all channelling PR to one high quality website with sales content. The following diagram may help explain this concept a bit more clearly:

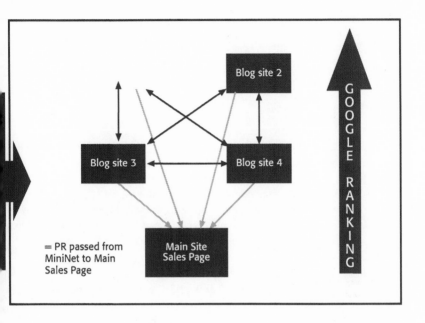

Many hosting companies allow you to install blogging software free. At www.GuerillaHosting.com you are able to install a number of different blogging applications to your site free and automatically. Once you have set up your administrator password, creating entries in your blog is as easy as typing a document in Microsoft Word.

Of all the free blogging applications, WordPress is probably the best and most popular. This can be installed from your CPanel in your GuerillaHosting. com account.

Remember, you will need to have your blog hosted on your own account for these tactics to work. If you use one of the free blogger sites like www.blogger. com you will not be in control of how you set up your blog mininet or where you point the PR.

eBay tactics.

"Tactics mean doing what you can with what you have"
Saul Alinsky

eBay gets serious traffic -- in fact, a whopping TWO MILLION eager buyers visit eBay every day, ready and willing to make purchases online.

And eBay is more than oddities and collectibles -- it's big, big business. In the first half of 2005, eBay members in the US alone sold over $10.6 billion dollars worth of goods to over 150 million registered users! Every serious Niche marketer should learn how to take advantage of these staggering statistics!

I have not traditionally marketed my books on Ebay, but have been conducting a lot of research of late. Don't get me wrong, I have been using Ebay for many years to buy and sell goods, but only now have I started to add Ebay to my arsenal of Niche Internet Marketing tactics.

I am currently conducting a series of experiments and research on the best ways to market your products and services on Ebay. All my findings will soon be available in a new ebook available at http://www.NicheInternetMarketing.com

As an existing customer, you will be entitled to a massive discount when purchasing this ebook, so keep your eyes peeled for the imminent release date.

Just to whet your appetite, here are some secrets I have already discovered.

- ALWAYS sell your items with a photo.

- ALWAYS provide quality feedback when buying or selling and request that the people you deal with provide feedback to you.

- ALWAYS provide accurate and fair pricing for postage and packaging.

- ALWAYS include a detailed description of the goods or service on offer.

- Make sure your product or service is listed in the correct category, and is listed in all the categories that people may be searching for it in.

- Make sure you follow up any queries from customers before the auction has ended.

- If you regularly stock the product you are selling, make the auction a dutch auction where you have a number of items for sale in the same auction.

- Including a 'Buy it now' price can encourage buyers to buy before the auction has ended.

- If the winning bidder fails to follow through with the purchase, be sure to offer the product to the second place bidder.

There are more detailed hints and tips to follow, and the results of my in depth analysis and experimentation, so stay tuned!

Action item! >>>

> Go to http://www.Ebay.com

> Browse through some of the auctions and observe how sellers have optimised their auction ads based on the guidelines above.

> Note which auctions have bids on them

Chapter 28

Alternative online and offline Niche methods for promoting your website.

"Method goes far to prevent trouble in business: for it makes the task easy, hinders confusion, saves abundance of time, and instructs those that have business depending, both what to do and what to hope."

William Penn

Okay, so you've mastered the search engines, tweaked your html, have a gazillion incoming links, have a massive opt-in email list that you email daily, have automated all your processes, have killer ad copy, have some great joint ventures, and have a healthy thriving internet business. So what else can you do to expand? How can you take your business to the next level? What kind of offline tactics can you use to get more exposure, more customers, and increase your bottom line? Below I have listed some of the best offline methods I have used to help gain exposure for my websites:

- Include your URL on all your business cards and stationary.
  Having a company or business URL not only looks professional, but people want to be able to quickly look up information about you without resorting to guessing your URL or searching in Google.

- Include your URL on all your company vehicles or you r personal vehicle if you are a sole trader.
  You will be surprised how many people remember a web address from a car, especially if it is short and memorable.

- Include your URL on any signage that are on external buildings or premises of your business.
  If you are on a busy road, there are potentially thousands of motorists driving past every day. Don't miss this opportunity to advertise your website.
- Have t-shirts and caps printed with all your URL that your staff can wear. Not only will this make your staff immediately identifiable as representatives of your company, but once again people will see and remember your web address. This is an especially useful tactic at trade-shows or when handing out leaflets for your company in busy pedestrian sites.

- Have pens, mouse mats and coffee mugs printed with your URL and hand these out to customers and potential customers. These items will be given prominent display on a desk, and will remain in the memory of the receiver.

- If you website topic is something that may be of interest to the local community, send a press release announcing your site to the local newspapers. If they are unwilling to publish your press release, request an interview, explaining the benefits of your product or service and how members of the local community would be interested in the information on your website.

- Have your URL printed on a giant inflatable.
  Giant inflatables have a unique fun factor to them. If for instance your business is for sporting goods, you could have a giant basketball with your web address printed across it. These inflatables can be seen for miles, and if erected for longer periods can even become local landmarks.

- If your site offers a very unique one-of-a-kind product or service you may be able to gain exposure through other media outlets such as TV and radio. Call around to your local studios and see if they'd be interested in running a spot on your new site.

- Have some employees or friends or relatives dress up (for instance with big afro wigs) and attend tv-televised sporting events wearing t-shorts with your URL printed on them. Get them to stand in prominent positions like behind the goalposts and cheer loudly when your team scores! The cameras often zoom-in on dressed up people for the novelty factor, especially if there are more than one of them.

- Create, or have created a funny flash cartoon featuring your URL. The novelty entertainment value of flash cartoons often means they are forwarded on and a viral effect is created. They'll be forwarded around to a large number of people in a short amount of time. Upload the flash cartoons to free download sites, and forward them to all your friends and colleagues.

- A Niche tactic employed by Vodafone in Australia was to have their logo painted across the back of a guy. At an appointed time during an international cricket match, the man with the logo on his back lost his shirt and ran onto the pitch. Eventually police caught him, and he was escorted away. However this was all caught on camera and aired live around the world. Vodafone paid the streaker's fine, but got worldwide tv coverage of their logo for the princely sum of $250! Although I don't recommend you break the law, this is an example of how being creative can return big results for a small or no outlay of money.

- If your product or service is localised, distribute business cards with your URL on them to your local area. Make sure you include some kind of discount or special offer for potential customers if they log on before a certain date. This will encourage them to take action.

- Take advantage of holidays periods (for example Christmas, Easter, Halloween, Thanksgiving, National Days) to offer special discounts to your customers. Remember these are the days people have off work and school and are likely to be at home surfing the net! Try to include a specialised holiday version of your logo (the way google does on holidays) so your potential customers know they will be getting a good deal because of the holiday. For example if it is Halloween, and your company name is "Noogle", make the 2 o's into pumpkins for your logo.

- Offer bonuses for ordering your product. Make sure the bonuses have a good value and are not just available anywhere else. If for instance you sell bread baking machines, you could include a free report with 20 bread recipes. People love bonuses, so make sure you highlight what the customer will be receiving when they order your product.

- Include a photo of yourself and/or your staff on your website. In the often depersonalised world that is the web, people like to see who they are dealing with. Not only will it give them more confidence to do business with you, but it is friendlier and gives the personal touch. So include photos of you and your staff on your website – even if it is only in the contact page.

- If you're selling an information product, for example an e-book, or a downloadable video or audio series, make sure you have professionally designed e-book, audio or video covers for your products. Not only does it look more professional, and portray the image that you are a serious company selling quality products, but it will increase your bottom line, as the graphics and wording on your e-book cover will encapsulate what the product is.

- Make it easy for your customers to order. Make your ordering system a simple one-click system where the buyer is directed to the payment page. Also make sure your buttons for ordering are displayed clearly and prominently throughout all of your web pages. The last thing people want to have to do is scroll up and down a whole lot of long copy to find the "Buy Now" button.

- Include photos, graphics and good descriptions of your product and service offerings. People want to be able to see and visualise what they are buying. They want exact specifications. How much does it weigh, what are its dimensions, what colour is it, what is it made from?

- If you have 2 major products or services that you sell, create a different site for each one, register a different URL for each product, then link the 2 sites to increase your PR and site rankings. The same can be done with 3, 4, 5 or more products. The sky is the limit, use your imagination.

- Survey your customers and find out exactly what it is that they want. Maybe you are offering the wrong type of product or service, or there are other products or services they would like to see bundled with yours! This is extra money you are missing out on! Find out, and then give your customers what they want.

Chapter 29

Web 2.0 – opportunities for the Niche Marketer

"Luck is what happens when preparation meets opportunity."

Seneca

With the advent of websites such as www.YouTube.com, www.FaceBook.com and www.MySpace.com, a plethora of cool new ways to market your products and services to both mass markets and niche groups of people has become available.

For the launch of his recent smash-hit book 'The 4-hour work week', Timothy Ferriss employed the use of Web 2.0 technologies to launch his book. A book launch of this magnitude had never before relied solely on free internet advertising to reach critical mass. However Ferriss employed the techniches to astounding success. Goto www.YouTube.com and do a search for '4 hour work week'. As well as finding all of the videos that have popped up since The 4-hour work week became a New York Times bestseller, you will also see some of the original promo films for the book.

Facebook.com has a feature that allows any member to create a group and allow members to join the group. Jim from www.JimsMemoryCards.com could create a 'Memory card' group in Facebook with a link back to his website. Photographers, gadget lovers and anybody interested in memory cards could join Jim's group to be amongst like-minded people, and to stay abreast of developments in the area. Facebook.com also allows an individual or company to program applications that are tightly integrated with Facebook and can be automatically downloaded and installed by members. Jim could create a memory card database or photo application within Facebook, and affiliate it with his memory card website.

So you don't know how to produce a video to upload to YouTube or create a Facebook application to increase exposure for your website? That doesn't matter; in the next chapter we'll cover outsourcing. Finding the right skills at the right price to take advantage of all the opportunities available.

Action item! >>>

> Go to www.FaceBook.com and conduct a search for 'memory card'. You will need to be a member, if you're not already – sign up, it's free!

> You'll notice there are currently no memory card groups or applications. This could be an untapped market for Jim!

> Go to www.YouTube.com and conduct a search for '4 hour work week'. Watch the 6 minute video entitled '4-Hour Workweek Video Summary + Highlights' – one of Timothy Ferriss' original marketing videos for his book.

> Now conduct a search for 'memory card'. Note there are quite a few videos already about memory cards. Most of these seem quite old. Jim could provide fresh new content about new memory cards and link these videos back to his website.

Chapter 30

Automating and Outsourcing – freeing up your time

For any website you start, the goal should always be to automate as much of the process as you can. From ordering to product fulfilment. From providing a forum for users to answer questions and queries amongst themselves and producing a quality FAQ section where answers to questions can be found 24/7 without emailing you. This is the way you need to structure your Niche Internet Marketing businesses. This allows you create one web property, lock and load, and then move onto the next. With this strategy, over time you will build up a portfolio of web businesses each bringing in multiple streams of income on auto-pilot.

Below is a list of things to keep in mind to ensure your website runs smoothly on auto-pilot:

- Have a quality FAQ section, and add questions and answers to those questions as you receive them over time.
- Have an auto-responder set up at your main email address that replies to any of your queries with the following information:

Thank-you for your email,

For any urgent questions you may have, please check our FAQ section at
http://www.JimsMemoryCards.com/FAQ.htm

You can also post a question at our forum, where there are many active members that will be able to give you a prompt and accurate reply:
http://www.JimsMemoryCards.com/forum

If you wish to check the status of your order, please contact XYZ delivery
company on 123 456 789 and quote your order reference number you
were given when ordering.

If you are interested in joining our email list to receive monthly updates
and specials on memory cards, please go here: http://www.JimsMemoryCards.com/newsletter.htm

For all other enquires, please be patient, this email address is checked on
Monday and Thursday at 11am, we will respond to your query then.

Regards,

Jim
http://www.JimsMemoryCards.com

This gives your customer all the information they may need to find the
answer to their query, and sets their expectation as to the timeframe in which
they can expect a reply.

- Always promote products that are part of an affiliate program, can be
  delivered electronically (software and informational products), or can
  be drop-shipped for you by the wholesaler. This ensures you will never
  have to worry about order fulfilment or returns. Authorise your wholesaler to process returns and issue refunds on your behalf without seeking your permission first. These returns can be settled at the end of
  each month when you place your new order.

- If you plan to be away or busy for a few months, either write a few issues ahead for your newsletter and set them up on an auto-responder, or delegate the task of writing and sending the newsletter to somebody else.

- Assign a moderator for your forum that will have additional privileges over the general forum user and will be able to monitor the content, and delete any offensive or inappropriate posts.

It is unlikely that with all the work you have to do in setting up your niche web business, that you will have all the skills required or time available to perform all the tasks required to make your website a success. That's why I am a huge fan of outsourcing. From website design, to article writing and submission and forum population – I outsource the lot! The internet has created a global economy where a lot of skilled labour is available for a relatively cheap price. You could have a Masters graduate from India writing articles for your website for $5 per hour. You could have a house-wife in Asia creating backlinks to your site for $3 per hour.

To browse the services available and the prices you could be paying visit the following sites:

http://www.YourManInIndia.com
http://www.b2kcorp.com

These companies will be able to provide you with a virtual assistant to perform almost any of the tasks required to get your niche web business off the ground and running – and making it a success.

If I have a specific project with clearly defined tasks and outcomes, I will post a project at one of the following sites:

http://www.elance.com
http://www.GetAFreelancer.com

For $5 you can post a project and have service providers coming back to you with bids for your project. You can send messages to potential service providers to clarify their skills and experience as well as view portfolios of their previous work. The layout and cover design of this book were created by sourcing services as described above!

Here is an example of a project I posted at GetAFreelancer.com for a virtual assistant:

Budget:	$30-100
Created:	01/20/2008 at 21:58 EST
Bidding Ends:	02/19/2008 at 21:58 EST

Description:

Hi there,

I require the services of a Virtual Assistant. This will be a long term engagement, I wish to build a relationship with one company, and have one excellent virtual assistant assigned to me with a team of back-up assistants.

I require this service to be billed on an hourly basis, however, I will ge gauging perfomance on output (speed to complete tasks), and the quality of the work produced.

My virtual assistant must have excellent written and spoken English, and may be required to make telephone calls as well.

The main tasks you will be required to perform include:

- Link building
- Forum commenting
- HTML setup, maintenance and design
- Blog setup, customisation, maintenance (Wordpress)
- Replying to emails
- Research (and associated report writing)
- formatting documents to certain specifications
- Article writing
- Simple banner design
- Replying to emails
- Basic Book-keeping
- Advertising sales
- Other tasks as required.

Please reply to this project with details of your company (name, physical address, website, certifications), security measures you employ to ensure data remains confidential and your employees are properly screened.

Please also include 3 references from current clients.
Please also include a Curriculum Vitae of the virtual assistant you propose assigning to me. Include all relevant experience and education details. The volume of work required to be completed will probably average 10 hours per week, so it is okay if my virtual assistant also looks after other clients, please let me know how many clients the VA you are proposing for my account will have. Please include examples of the work completed by this

specific virtual assistant (reports, articles, and info on other projects completed.)

Please also include brief details on the backup team of VAs, and how the team is managed. I am Australian based, so will require work to be done in a timely manner which may occasionaly include 24/7 service for urgent work. Deadlines will generally be tight with 24 hours to complete projects.

Please indicate your hourly rate for this virtual assistant position. Keeping in mind that this will vary per week, but will probably average 10 hours per week.

I look forward to working with the successful service provider and virtual assistant.

Here are the replies I received:

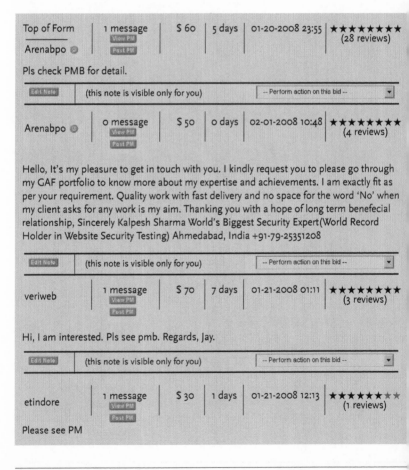

| Top of Form ——— Arenabpo ◉ | 1 message View PM Post PM | $ 60 | 5 days | 01-20-2008 23:55 | ★★★★★★★★★ (28 reviews) |

Pls check PMB for detail.

| Edit Note | (this note is visible only for you) | -- Perform action on this bid -- ▼ |

| Arenabpo ◉ | 0 message View PM Post PM | $ 50 | 0 days | 02-01-2008 10:48 | ★★★★★★★★★ (4 reviews) |

Hello, It's my pleasure to get in touch with you. I kindly request you to please go through my GAF portfolio to know more about my expertise and achievements. I am exactly fit as per your requirement. Quality work with fast delivery and no space for the word 'No' when my client asks for any work is my aim. Thanking you with a hope of long term benefecial relationship, Sincerely Kalpesh Sharma World's Biggest Security Expert(World Record Holder in Website Security Testing) Ahmedabad, India +91-79-25351208

| Edit Note | (this note is visible only for you) | -- Perform action on this bid -- ▼ |

| veriweb | 1 message View PM Post PM | $ 70 | 7 days | 01-21-2008 01:11 | ★★★★★★★★★ (3 reviews) |

Hi, I am interested. Pls see pmb. Regards, Jay.

| Edit Note | (this note is visible only for you) | -- Perform action on this bid -- ▼ |

| etindore | 1 message View PM Post PM | $ 30 | 1 days | 01-21-2008 12:13 | ★★★★★★★☆☆ (1 reviews) |

Please see PM

| ajwassoc ◎ | 2 message [View PM] [Post PM] | $ 100 | 30 days | 01-20-2008 22:38 | (No Feedback Yet) |

See PM for details.

| rvsekar2000 | 2 message [View PM] [Post PM] | $30 | 3 days | 01-21-2008 02:30 | (No Feedback Yet) |

Sir, Sub: Wanted Virtual Assistant Position I am from India. time zone Greenwich time + 5.30 hrs . I am having corporate and financial accounting, legal drafting, Company secretarial work (drafting board minutes, general body meeting, legal drafting) for more than 25 years. My educational qualifications are as follows: 1. Masters in Commerce. 2. Associate member of the Institute of Chartered Secretaries and Administrators. (UK). 3. Fellow Member of the Indian Institute of Company Secretaries, New Delhi. 4. LLB degree. I am having my own lab tap and broadband connection and available for communication through skype or yahoo messenger. I am well versed in MS Office and can present any MIS. I am a regular writer of dissertation, essay on Economics, Accounting, Law, finance and general topics I can handle independently the following any of the positions: ü Having accurate typing skills ü Preparation of legal documents. ü General office work, document preparation. ü Enter data, type reports and numeric data. ü -bookkeeping, financial document prep- I am having more than 25 experience in accounting field I request you to admit me as your virtual assistant as I am capable of providing quality and time bound services. My minimum quote is $750 per month. Regards, R.V.Seckar

| assistant4u2008 | 0 message [View PM] [Post PM] | $ 50 | 7 days | 01-21-2008 03:01 | (No Feedback Yet) |

Hello, I'm very interested in working with you. I'm an experienced virtual administrative assistant. Thanks, assistant4u2008

| workglobal | 0 message [View PM] [Post PM] | $ 100 | 7 days | 01-21-2008 03:50 | (No Feedback Yet) |

I can help you with what you want, I can work on part or full time basis and willing to sign a non-discloure agreement. Thank you.

| deseret | 0 message / View PM / Post PM | $ 100 | 5 days | 01-21-2008 10:13 | (No Feedback Yet) |

i have severals years in this kind of job. I am an administrative assistant certified. Just let me know when I can start. regards

| seopractices | 1 message / View PM / Post PM | $ 100 | 5 days | 01-21-2008 10:20 | (No Feedback Yet) |

Thanks for posting the Job offer. Please check PM for details.

| hauf | 0 message / View PM / Post PM | $ 100 | 7 days | 01-23-2008 05:35 | (No Feedback Yet) |

I'm interested in your project. Thanks

| janinemilbradt | 0 message / View PM / Post PM | $ 39 | 2 days | 01-23-2008 19:24 | (No Feedback Yet) |

Experienced Excel/ Access user. Flexible schedule and fast service. Eduation and experience. I have a Masters of Science in Management and a B.S. in Accounting and Business Administration: Finance.

| amira222 | 0 message / View PM / Post PM | $ 100 | 20 days | 01-24-2008 18:49 | (No Feedback Yet) |

Dear Sir, I am English native speaker, live in Slovakia. I am able to start working right away. I am willing to send you my full resume, upon your response. Thank you Shaimaa Andrassy

| thivankasl | 0 message / View PM / Post PM | $ 30 | 5 days | 01-25-2008 00:38 | (No Feedback Yet) |

Dear sir, Please visit our web site www.convenient.info

	(this note is visible only for you)			-- Perform action on this bid --	▼

JFEMarketing	0 message View PM Post PM	$ 30	1 days	01-25-2008 18:30	(No Feedback Yet)

Hello, I'll work for you for 2 weeks at 10 hours a week for FREE. After that, I would just like a letter of recommendation from you telling future employers of my work. Let me know. -Andy

	(this note is visible only for you)			-- Perform action on this bid --	▼

amandamarie	1 message View PM Post PM	$ 100	7 days	01-31-2008 07:23	★★★★★★★★ (4 reviews)

Hello from West Virginia! I'm very excited to place my bid toward becoming your Virtual Assistant and bringing increased productivity to the table. I have a great amount of experience to offer as well as a great education and the 'go getter' attitude that is needed for quality work to be accomplished. I perform remote secretarial services because I enjoy helping professionals become more organized and less stressed. My education includes an associate degree in computer engineering, the Microsoft Office Master Specialist certification (Access, Outlook, PowerPoint, Word and Excel Expert Tests Passed) as well as several other computer related certifications (MCP, CompTIA A+, CompTIA Network+, Train-the-Trainer). The applications in Microsoft Office are part of my daily routine and I'm very skilled in that area. I've taught Microsoft Office in several colleges throughout West Virginia. In my work history, I have obtained 8 years of administrative office experience. Together, administrative and technical familiarities enable me to work efficiently on a variety of tasks. In a short period of time you'll come to rely on me as your consistent catch-all! My home office is organized in a manner that will serve you well. I take pride in my work. Whether it is a complex task or a simple ToDo, I have the desire and motivation to do a good job in all my labors. Since work is carried out at a distance, I put forth a strong effort at all times to maintain good communication. This means you'll never be in the dark about the status of your tasks as I will be keeping you up to date. I'm confident in saying I can meet and exceed your expectations. You'll be pleased to find that my skills in business correspondence are outstanding both written and verbal. My phone etiquette is also above average. I'm sure you'll enjoy the synergy that can be established in a short period of time as my personality comes well-received. My bid is based on 10hrs of labor each week at the rate of $10 per hour. However, I can provide up to forty hours each week if needed. I look forward to learning more about your business and how I can contribute to its success! I can begin immediately! Attached you will find my resume and office specs for further consideration. Sincerely, Amanda Silverman

	(this note is visible only for you)			-- Perform action on this bid --	▼

free2dil99	0 message View PM Post PM	$ 80	26 days	02-11-2008 03:41	(No Feedback Yet)

Many of the potential service providers were willing to work for $2-$3 per hour and in one case a VA offered to work for free for 2 weeks in return for a written reference!

Another great source of good cheap content, services and products for your niche web business is the Warrior Special Offer forums. Go here to check it out: http://www.warriorforum.com/forum/forum.asp?FORUM_ID=15 You can often find deals for #30 to get a whole website created, or similar prices for unique PLR (Private label rights) content.

In pure economic terms, if I can earn $30 an hour with my employer, then I can afford to pay somebody $5 per hour for 10 hours per month to work on a website that is producing over $2000 in profits per month. That frees up my spare time to pursue other interests or spend time with my family. It just makes sense.

Action item! >>>

> Go to http://www.GetAFreelancer.com

> Set up an account and post a project.

> Get a service provider to write some articles for you based on your selected topic, get your website designed, or build some backlinks to your existing website.

> Go to the Warrior Special Offer forums and browse the current offers:
http://www.warriorforum.com/forum/forum.asp?FORUM_ID=15

> If you are ready to have your website designed or purchase some PLR articles for content for your site, then make some purchases! All providers accept Paypal as payment.

Chapter 31

U seful Tools –
Great tools to help you design and promote an optimised web site.

"We shall neither fail nor falter; we shall not weaken or tire...give us the tools and we will finish the job."

Winston Churchill

Nichebot – www.nichebot.com

Internet Marketing Magazine – www.websitemarketingmagazine.com

Internet Marketing Toolbar – http://www.websitemarketingtoolbar.com/

Overture Search Term Suggestion Tool – http://inventory.overture.com/d/searchinventory/suggestion/

Google Toolbar – http://toolbar.google.com/en_GB/

Alexa Toolbar – http://download.alexa.com

Zeus, the Internet Marketing robot – http://www.cyber-robotics.com

Clipmate – http://www.clipmate.com

Traffic Swarm – http://www.trafficswarm.com

Your Man In India - http://www.YourManInIndia.com

Brickwork - http://www.b2kcorp.com

Elance - http://www.elance.com

Get a Freelancer - http://www.GetAFreelancer.com

ClickBank – http://www.Clickbank.com

Commission Junction – http://www.cj.com

Chapter 32

U seful Resources –
Great reference material to help you make your site a success.

"The courage to imagine the otherwise is our greatest resource, adding color and suspense to all our life."

James Thurber

Gorilla Internet Marketing – http://www.glenncanady.com

Derek Gehl's Internet Marketing – http://www.marketingtips.com

Michael Campbell's Revenge of the mininet – http://www.revengeofthemininet.com

Create your own toolbar – http://websitemarketingtoolbar.com/customtoolbar.html

Cheap Domain Name Registration – www.Godaddy.com

Cheap Web Design Templates – 100 Web Templates – free trial http://www.regnow.com/trialware/download/Download_100webs. exe?item=10557-11&affiliate=61321

Cheap Hosting – http://www.GuerillaHosting.com

Affiliate Marketing Software – Instant Affiliate Pro http://www.regnow.com/ softsell/nph-softsell.cgi?item=10675-1&affiliate=61321

Ebook Creation Software – EbookMaker FREE trial download http://www.regnow.com/trialware/download/Download_ebookmaker. exe?item=8527-8&affiliate=61321

Submit your site to Google – http://www.google.co.uk/addurl/?hl=en&continue=/addurl

Submit your site to Yahoo – http://search.yahoo.com/info/submit.html

Submit your site to DMOZ – http://dmoz.org/add.html

Cheap Spybot and Adware removal – NoAdware – FREE trial download
http://www.regnow.com/trialware/download/Download_noadware.
exe?item=12536-1&affiliate=61321

Magazine Template – http://www.Magazine-Template.com

Amazon – www.Amazon.com

YouTube – www.YouTube.com

Facebook – www.FaceBook.com

Ebay – www.Ebay.com

Chapter 33

Suggested Reading

"Reading makes a full man; conference a ready man;
and writing an exact man."
Sir Francis Bacon

The Long Tail – Chris Anderson

The 4-Hour Work Week – Timothy Ferriss

The Tipping Point – Malcolm Gladwell

Blink - Malcolm Gladwell

The Google Story – David Vise

Microtrends – Mark J. Penn

Million dollar Consulting – Alan Weiss

The Attractor Factor – Joe Vitale

The Wisdom of Crowds - James Surowiecki

Action item! >>>

> Read at least one good book per month. Educate yourself, expand your horizons, and fulfil your dreams!

Chapter 34

What now?

"Our life is composed greatly from dreams, from the unconscious,
and they must be brought into connection with action.
They must be woven together."

Anais Nin

So you have made it this far, you have read my entire book. Well now the ball is in your court my friend. What you now do with this information is up to you. Hopefully you have some ideas about the kind of niche internet business you want to start, or the product or service you want to sell. If you don't, don't worry! You can start off by selling somebody else's product or service and earning a nice commission!

Niche Internet Marketing is intended to be a reference guide for you as you make your progress through the initial creation, and eventual running of your internet business. As new techniques become available online, and old techniques cease to work, you will be hearing from me through my newsletter, and updates of this book.

Refer back to this book often; it is intended to provide both a source of inspiration, and a convenient collection of all the resources and information you will need to run your internet business successfully.

What I suggest you do first is sit down and write down the goals you wish to achieve with your internet business. Where do you want to be in 6 months, 1 year, 3 years and 5 years? Be explicit in the detail of your goals. Write what they are and how you are going to achieve them. Next you will need to write down your action plan for achieving your goals. This is a more detailed step by step plan which details exactly what you are going to do, how you are going to do it, and the timescale in which you expect to complete that phase of your plan.

Now all that is left is to get started. Don't be scared about taking that first step towards your niche internet business and dreams. Often the initial dipping of your toe in the water can be the scariest part. But it can also be the most exciting and exhilarating part of the whole journey. You are going into the unknown; you are setting out to achieve your dreams. Don't ever be afraid of this, everybody had to start at the beginning at some point, and it is never too late, this is your journey, you are seeking your own destiny! Get out there and have a go. Show the world what you are made of. You may be so wildly successful in such a short period of time, that you will even astound yourself. Never waiver from your plans and goals. Work steadily towards them. If people tell you it can't be done, then find somebody who says it can be done because they have done it! Get them to show you how they did it, and then copy what they did. If it has never been done before, then find somebody who believes in you and associate with them, find out new ways to achieve your goals.

I also provide a number of consulting and support services. If you need any of the following services, please send me an email and we can discuss how I can help fast track your internet business success:

COPYWITING (PER PRODUCT / PAGE)
100 Incoming Links
300 Incoming Links
500 Incoming Links
Website Setup and design (including e-commerce and hosting)
Creation of Customised Toolbar
Logo Design
Yahoo and Google Submission Guaranteed
Adwords Campaign
Re-design of Website
Business Plan for Web Business
Speaking engagements

To enquire about any of the above services, contact me here: http://www.NicheInternetMarketing.com and click the 'Contact' tab.

Either myself or one of my friendly staff will reply promptly to your query.

And don't forget my other great Internet Marketing resources:

Internet Marketing Magazine – www.websitemarketingmagazine.com

Internet Marketing Toolbar – http://www.websitemarketingtoolbar.com

Guerilla Hosting – http://www.guerillahosting.com

If you're planning a trip to Thailand, you might also want to visit my Thailand accommodation site. It's secure, reliable and cheap – I use this site when booking accommodation myself! Drop me a line if you're going, we might be able to catch up for a drink!

http://www.Accommodation-Thailand.com

I also have a number of other exciting projects currently in progress. I'll keep you updated via my website as these come online!

Keep an eye on 5 of my latest upcoming projects which are currently in the final stages of implementation:

Ipod accessories, Skype phones, GPS navigation, outsourcing and how to launch your own product.

These sites will take advantage of 2 of the hottest products and technologies on the market today. Keep an eye on them regularly, and you will see how the sites evolve.

I am also excited to hear about all your new success stories. I live and breathe this stuff. So when you have a success by applying my methods, make sure you let me know. You can contact me here: http://www.NicheInternet Marketing.com Click on the 'Contact' tab and leave a message.

To all your Niche Internet Marketing success!

Good Luck and god bless.

Leigh Burke.
http://www.NicheInternetMarketing.com

BONUS Chapters:

1. Goto http://nicheinternetmarketing.com/?page_id=12

2. Enter the password as directed (it is a word from this book).

3. Download and enjoy!

Chapter 35

NICHE Internet Marketing Case Studies

Brent Crouch from www.BrentCrouch.com

1. **What was your first web business?**

   Jillian Distributors

   http://www.JillianDistributors.com

   I started this site to sell imported products to retail businesses.

2. **When did you start this?**

   11/2001

3. **How much time did you devote to setting this up and running it?**

   When I first created this site, I was already selling product on eBay. My wife and I devoted 20 - 30 hours a week to getting the site off the ground. As time went on, we spent more time not less. The year that I grew this business from 200K to 670K, I spent 2 – 3 days working with no sleep. I don't miss those days at all!

4. **How much did it cost to set up and run?**

   It cost me less than $300 to start this site. This includes domain registration, hosting, and shopping cart.

5. **How much money did you make?**

   That first year in business, we had a total of $25,000 in sales. In December of 2005, we had our first $10,000 month. I couldn't believe it. I thought we had arrived! In December of 2007, I had more than $200,000 in sales for December and gross revenue of 1.25 million dollars for the year.

6. **What were the biggest challenges in setting up and running this web business?**

   Everything was a challenge. I knew nothing about building websites when I started. The first site revision was terrible and is still available at archive.org. I didn't even have a shopping cart. Customer's had to type and email a list of the products they wanted. Very inefficient.

7. What happened to the web business?

   The site grew beyond anything I ever imagined. A few years ago, we had to purchase a warehouse. Once you are getting tractor trailers everyday, it isn't practical to work out of the house anymore.

   Today, we have 8 employees that help us run the business.

8. **Please provide any URLs / screenshots or other promo literature (sales page etc.)**

    http://www.jilliandistributors.com

    http://www.smallbusinesscomputing.c....php/2176641

9. **What is your background?**

    My background is in electrical engineering. My wife, Priscilla, has a background in accounting and customer service.

10. **Did your background help with this web business in anyway**

    Yes and no. I had no idea how the web worked, but my engineering background made me a natural information gatherer and problem solver.

11. **What did you learn from this first web business?**

    I've learned everything from SEO, PPC, customer service, marketing skills, employee management, and business law. I've learned more than I ever wanted to know about income taxes and accounting systems.

12. **What web businesses fo you run now?**

    I am in the process of building a network for quality information sites monetized with adsense. Two blogs I own are brentcrouch.com and blogrepreneur.com

13. **When did you start this?**

    I've started building other sites about 2 years ago.

14. **How much time did you devote to setting this up and running it?**

    I spend over 60 - 70 hours a week running my web businesses. My wife also spends 24 - 32 hours working in the business.

15. **How much did it cost to set up and run?**

    I pay $50 a month for a VPS from Servint.net. When I want to start a new website, my only expense is domain registration and any custom graphics I want to add to the site.

16. **How much money do you make?**

    I've tripled my salary as an engineer with my web businesses.

17. **What were the biggest challenges in setting up and running this web business?**

    The biggest problems are sorting the fact from the hype. The internet is a little like the wild west. There is someone selling snake oil on every corner. If you are going to succeed you have to be smart enough to determine fact from fiction.

    The internet can be a tough nut to crack. Most people fail before they even start. If you want to guarantee success in this business, you have to refuse to fail and be stubborn enough to keep your word.

18. **What are your top 5 goals for this web business?**

    I am in the process of working with my CPA to prepare this business for sale. It's been a wild ride and very rewarding, but I am interested in pursuing other web projects.

19. **What top 5 tips would you give to somebody starting a business online?**

Don't give up. I felt like I was wasting my time so many times when I was starting. Obviously, I couldn't have been more wrong.

Work hard. If you are dreaming of drinking fruity drinks on the beach while checks roll in, well that isn't reality for most of us. I do play hard, but I work harder.

Do something you love doing.

Get started now!

Set goals.

20. **Do you plan to start any more web businesses in the next 24 months? If so, what are the details?**

I have a pretty big project in the works right now. I don't want to give out a lot of details. I will say it is based on the eBay affiliate program and approaches the program in a way I haven't seen anyone else do.

It will be a big success or a big failure. Only time and testing will tell.

21. **What top 10 products or services would you recommend to somebody starting out online?**

Perry Marshalls -Guide to Google Adwords

Derek Gehl - Insider's Secrets to Marketing your Business on the Internet http://www.marketingtips.com/tipslt...IPSCLICKS002

Rosalind Gardner – Super Affiliate Handbook
http://netprofitstoday.com/index.php

Charlie Page – Directory of Ezines
http://directoryofezines.com/

Robert Allen – Multiple Streams of Internet Income
http://www.amazon.com/Multiple-Stre...p/0471410144

22. **Do you have any role models or mentors? If so, who are they, and how did you get them?**

One of the guys I talk to most and share ideas with is Josh Spaulding of ez-onlinemoney.com. I met Josh by being a frequent commentor on his blog.

23. **What are you top 3 favourite reasons for running an online business? (E.g flexible hours, run my own business, access to global markets etc.)**

Money, money, money

24. **Any final words?**

Do something! I talk to a lot of people I know that are interested in duplicating my success. The problem is they are too afraid to take the first step. You can't spend years learning and asking questions. That's all good, but I learned more by making mistakes and then working and searching for information to correct them.

I didn't know you couldn't start a 1.2 million dollar business in a two car garage, so I did it! You can do the same thing.

■ **Avery Berman, the 18 year old success story**
http://www.SuperSuccessfulSecrets.com

1. **What was your first web business?**

   Now this is a tough question. You could say my first web business was at the age of 13. I played a video game called "The Sims Online." In this game there were thousands of players who were connected and playing with each other at the same time. I learned quickly that I was really good (like, REALLY good) at making money in the game. Browsing eBay one day, I realized I was able to sell my "fake" money, for REAL money! So... I did! I made probably about $1,000 doing this. However this wasn't a business. It was just a 13 year old experimenting with video games and ebay!

   My first real web business was really acting as an affiliate. I wrote articles and had affiliate links in them so I would earn commissions.

   It was very slow, and not much money was coming in. It wasn't until I started founding my own products and websites that I stared making real money.

   I'd say my first real website was selling a guide on how to keep fat off of your pets. I learned many valuable lessons from this website, which later brought me much, much more profit in separate experiments. You can still see that site here: www.MyPetIsFat.com (Cool name, huh?)

2. **When did you start this?**

   I'd say this site was started up around October of 2007.

3. **How much time did you devote to setting this up and running it?**

   I was working on many things at the time, but speicfially that site really didn't take up very much of my time. A few hours a week, maybe. However, at this stage I was spening many, many hours a day working on many different projects. (I didn't know it yet, but they were going to bring the real money!)

4. **How much did it cost to set up and run?**

   Incredibly cheap. I already had a host at $80/year. I spent $10 to buy the domain, I got a free Private Label Rights product which I rewrote and I got the graphics professionally done by a very skiller designer in exchange for a testimonial. My entire costs? A good chunk of my time and about $90.

5. **How much money did you make?**

That page made a few hundred net. I started to see red after a bit with advertising though, as it is hard to keep such a cheap product (I was selling the book for about $10) afloat... ESPCAILLY when you aren't really passionate about the product. I'd say that was my biggest lesson from this first project... you have to be passionate about what you are selling to really make it work!

6. **What were the biggest challenges in setting up and running this web business?**

The biggest challeges were really figuring out how to get it advertised, how to write the sales page, how to create the graphics, how best to price the product, what to offer with it... since it was my first real experiance, it was all farily new to me. I had the skills, it was just my first real test of implementation!

7. **What happened to the web business?**

I still own that site, but I'm not doing anything with it. It's just sitting in cyberspace, not making a penny. I'm considering going back to it and making it all shiny and new, improving the sales page, the product... pretty much everything. With the knowledge I have now, I have no doubts that I can turn that into a profitable page. I just have to decide if I really want to spend time on a product that I'm not very passionate about...

8. **Please provide any URLs / screenshots or other promo literature (sales page etc.)**

You can see this first site still at www.MyPetIsFat.com. Really my favorite part of that site is the graphics. I still can't believe I got them for free!

That main site is actually a "squeeze page," or a page where I collect email addresses. To see the actual sales letter, check out this site: www.MyPetIsFat.com/diet.htm

9. **What is your background?**

My background? Good question. I have no idea where I get it! Seriously though, I think most of my entreupenorial spirit comes from my Dad. He ran his own businesses when he was my age as well. I suppose he had an influence on how I thought about things. As far as how I grew up (hey, I'm still growing up!

I'm only 18 years old!) I was a solid B student until my Jr year in High School, at which point I turned things up a notch and became a straight A student.

I played a lot of video games in my youth as well, and thought I wanted to be an IT person when I grew up. It was through this that I becaome very knowledgable about computers. I just did something drastically different with them than I originally intended! I am currently enrolled in Ulster County Community College taking a custom major emphasizing (you guessed it!) business.

10. Did your background help with this web business in anyway?

My background did have some aid in my business. Mainly the fact that I was extremely familiar with computers and the Internet helped. I'd say the only other factor would have to be the sublimial influence my dad must have over me! Like father like son.

11. What did you learn from this first web business?

I'd say the most important thing I learned from this first site is that aside from basic web site creation, advertising and other basics you need to know, I need to have a passion for what I'm selling to really be successful. It wasn't until I stared working on things that I genuinly cared about did I really start making the big bucks!

12. What web businesses do you run now?

I ran several other sites between then and now (I know, hard to believe right? At the time of this writing, that was only 5 months ago!) all of which made me more and more profit. However, right now I'd say my favorite and most profitable business is my "Super Successful Secrets of Internet Marketing" book. This book is dedicated to helping others reach the same success I have, and it goes over the exact same things I do in my own business to make thousands every week.

This site is my baby, and I am constantly adding new things to it and I actually get emails from people who have started making money using my techniques. This is absolute favorite and most profitable site, as I am extremely passionate about the subject and love helping people make money online. You can see this site here:

www.SuperSuccessfulSecrets.com. Sign up when you get there! I have a very cool video where I explain juicy details about how much I make and the full story about how I got started online. (It's very cool!)

13. When did you start this?

I started this site in February of 2008, and as I already stated, it is far and away my favorite project, as well as my most profitable site.

14. How much time did you devote to setting this up and running it?

I did and still do spent a LOT of my time on this site. But it's fun for me so the time just flies by! I am contantly responding to emails, making new videos, adding new content, recording new audios, making tweaks to the webpage among other tasks. I'd say I spend a good few hours at least on it every day, but it feels like nothing! When I first was setting it up, however, I'd say I spent a good 6-10 hours a day on it. (It wasn't any less fun, though!)

15. How much did it cost to set up and run?

To set up the site, it was about the same as all my others. $10 for registration, and about $80 a year for hosting. Since I'm using that hosting service for several other websites as well, I don't count that $80 as really being the full expense! So, it was even cheaper to set up than the last one!

I wrote the product myself, the sales page, all the videos... I did everything myself. All it took was my time. But it was FUN for me, so it wasn't a big deal! (How awesome is that?)

16. How much money do you make?

Now this is a question I thought was private! (At least that's what I grew up thinking.) But since you asked, I'd be happy to give you an idea. At the time of this writing, March 22nd 2008, I'm currently earning over $4,000 a month, and it is growing almost every week. (By the time you read this I will probably be making much more!) In fact, two days ago I had my best "sleep income" to date. I woke up to over $700 dollars just waiting for me to spend! Today so far I've made over $500. As a matter of fact, I've made over $4,200 in the past 14 days! You know what the coolest part about all this is? I'm only 18.

17. What were the biggest challenges in setting up and running this web business?

Really the biggest challenges for my current major web business was, and still is, finding the best advertising methods. There are so many different ways you can go, and I'm experimenting with all I can. Personally, I love making videos, so YouTube and other video sites have been my friend. But all in all, the biggest challenge is finding a source of continuous, predictable, interested traffic.

18. What are your top 5 goals for this web business?

Hmmm. Interesting question. I'd have to say the following, in no particular order, are my top 5 current goals for "Super Successful Secrets."

1) Get to the front page of the Clickbank Marketplace for my catagories. (Clickbank is the third party processor which takes payments for me, and has a marketplace set up for their top publishers.)
2) have my site known as "an authority figure."
3) Have a $10,000 day from this site alone.
4) Get the site on autopilot through affiliate promotion.
5) Help the name "Avery Berman" become synomimous with "young successful Internet marketer." (and "totally awesome guy," but that's another story!)

19. What top 5 tips would you give to somebody starting a business online?

This is easy. I get asked this kind of question a lot. (Usually from my jealous friends!) Here are my top 5 tips, from least to most important.

5) Educate yourself on the subject before jumping in. It's easy to lose a lot of money if you don't know what you're doing.

4) After you get educated a bit... STOP! This isn't to say that you should stop getting educated (in fact you should NEVER stop!) but you need to learn when you have enough information to go on. One of the biggest reasons people fail is because they simply don't stop learning. So, they "know it all," but they aren't making anything. They get "information overload" and can't stop thinking of ideas, but they don't act on any of them. DON'T LET THIS HAPPEN TO YOU!

3) Network with others. Join forums dedicated to Internet marketing, talk with other business people, email successful people... do whatever you need to in order to get talking with other marketers. I can honestly say that most of my success would not have happened had it not been for networking with others and sharing ideas.

2) Do something that you are passionate about. If you are creating or marketing any product, your own or otherwise, make sure you love it. Make sure it is something that you LIKE to talk about and do. This will make the "work" FUN, and the income will just start to flow in from all over when you are working with something you love.

1) KNOW YOU ARE GOING TO BE SUCCESSFUL! Yes, that's right.. even on day one you need to know that you are going to make it! It's really not very hard.

You just need to sit down and tell yourself. "Self, I'm going to make thousands of dollars online and quit my job." And you know what? If you tell yourself this and believe it, it will happen. I honestly and truly believe this, and I use this thinking technique every day. I still tell myself every single day that I'm going to make more and more money and reach greater and greater success. And you know something? I do. So realize you're going to make it big, despite what anyone else days, despite even what you really think! Here's a secret for you, too... you really CAN do it! We all can!

0) Yes, that's right, I added one. Here is a bonus tip for you, no charge. This one tip I'd say is the most important tip I could ever give... ever. In fact I frequently tell people this almost every day, and I know if they listen, they will be forced to reach success. NEVER GIVE UP! Yup, that's it. Do not EVER give up. No matter what happens, do not stop. THE ONLY WAY YOU CAN POSSIBLY FAIL, IS IF YOU STOP TRYING! If you never let defeat rear its ugly head, you will be forced to succeed. I promise. Never give up. Never give in. You can do it.

You really can. And you really will!

20. Do you plan to start any more web businesses in the next 24 months? If so, what are the details?

Absolutely! I plan to create several other sites on various other topics, as well as Joint Venture with other marketers like myself. I already have two in the works. However, they are secret at the moment so I have to keep it on the down low! I like to work under pen names so no one can find everything I sell with a simple Google search and start to copy me! What I can tell you is that most of my sites will be following the information formula. I create a digital book full of incredibly valuable information and sell it. However, for one of my sites I'm working on with a friend, we are selling a program. I can't tell the specifics yet, but it should be very cool.

21. What top 10 products or services would you recommend to somebody starting out online?

I have a couple things that I think every single person who wants to make real money online needs to have.

1) Hosting. There just really isn't a feasible way to make predictable, steady, massive income without your own website and host. It's only about $80 a year, depending on where you go. I'd recommend Hostgator or Hostmonster.

2) An HTML editor. Now that you've got your host... you need to supply it with a site! Just a basic HTML editor is all you need. Frontpage and Dreamweaver are good options, but there are free ones you can download online that are quality as well.

3) FireFTP. You need an FTP service in order to actually get your site out there, and after trying a whole bunch of them, my far and away favorite is FireFTP.

   It's an addon for the Firefox browser (which you SHOULD be using) while is defintiely one of the friendliest interfaces and systems I've used.

4) You need to become a member of the Warrior Forum. This is a FREE community of likeminded Internet Marketers, and it is extremely active at all hours of the day. Honestly, the information in that forum is worth nothing short of millions. If you want to make money online, this should be your first step...

   just make sure you don't get information overload!

5) An autoresponder. This really is a must. This is a service that lets you collect names and email addresses (or any other information you may want) and email them whenever you need to. This is an invaluable marketing tool, and is definitly an asset you do not want to go

without when you get serious.

6) A payment processor. When you get to creating your own products or even being an affiliate, you will need to get a hold of a payment processor. The current largest for sending and accepting money is PayPal, however there are other options. There are also third parties such as Clickbank and PayDotCom who collect money for you and also allow affiliates to easily find your product so they can help promote it. This is definitly a very valuable situation, one which I'm currently taking advantage of in Clickbank.

7) Super Successful Secrets of Internet Marketing! Yes, it's my own product, but I honestly do believe it is the greatest way for anybody new to the game to get started with a great blueprint and a great plan to get started making real money online! I get unsolicited testimonials from people who have read it almost every week, and it's so great to know that I am helping people. If you are interested, I implore you to visit www.SuperSuccessfulSecrets.com.

22. Do you have any role models or mentors? If so, who are they, and how did you get them?

Now this is a tough question... I never really had any role models, and I still don't. I guess you can say that I've always sort of seen myself aspiring to reach equal and greater heights as Frank Kern and Mike Filsaime have reached. I suppose they are the closet things to role models I have.

Overall though, I just do my thing. I'm kinda my own role model. I don't let myself NOT reach greater successes.

23. What are you top 3 favourite reasons for running an online business?

This one's real easy. My top 3 favorite reasons for running my own business (and being self-employed) are:

1) I get to work when I want, where I want, and how much I want.

2) I have unlimited income potential. There's nothing stopping me from having a 5 million dollar day if I set out to do it. Maybe I will!

3) It's FUN! I love the work I do, and I get to do it to make my living. How cool is that?

There really is nothing better than being able to wake up when I want and start doing something I love while making more money than most people with '9-5' jobs. That's not to say I don't work hard, however. I do work very hard, but I just LIKE doing it!

24. Any final words?

You can do it. Seriously. You CAN do it... and you know something else? You WILL do it! You just have to KNOW THAT YOU WILL BE SUCCESSFUL! Never give up. The only way you will ever fail is if you stop trying. So

don't stop trying! I have a quote up on my wall by Henry Ford.
It reads "Whether you think that you can, or that you can't, you are ususally right." This statement can not be more true. You can do, you will do it...go to it!

Just promise to let me know when you've reached your wildest dreams...

Farah www.malaylingua.com
1. **What was your first web business?**
   MalayLingua Translation Services
   website : www.malaylingua.com
   It is a translation services web business which also includes proofreading, copywriting and reviewing various documents, manuals, terms, certificates, etc.
   I've started by specializing only on Eng-Malay language pairs and currently have more than 20 languages all around the world.
2. **When did you start this?**
   I've started on July 2003
3. **How much time did you devote to setting this up and running it?**
   For first 3 months, I took average of 5 hours daily for setting up. Once setup, it takes more than 6 hours for running the business i.e. marketing, send quote, completing project within project duration.
4. **How much did it cost to set up and run?**
   For hosting setup- domain registration, web design, logo creation, web hosting, estimated cost is $200 and another $50 for yearly maintenance.
   For vocation - certified member of translation board, courses and training, estimated cost is $700.
5. **How much money did you make?**
   My net gain is around $200-$500 a month.
6. **What were the biggest challenges in setting up and running this web business?**
   The biggest challenge that I'd faced when running up the business is to market the business and win the bidding project from clients. For setting up, I don't have any difficulties as the hosting services is available on the net and easy to get/buy.
7. **What happened to the web business?**
   I still owned and run the website.
8. Please provide any URLs / screenshots or other promo literature
   http://www.clarelibrary.ie/eolas/library/services/book-promos/promos.htm
9. **What is your background?**

I'm a Master's graduates in Network Engineering doing researches and analysis. My hobbies are surfing internet, reading books. I'm a mother of 2 lovely daughters and a good housewife who make home-based on line businesses.

10. **Did your background help with this web business in any way?**

    Yes it help. In the sense of my research on IT/telecommunications area I got the idea of doing the web business during studying and completing my thesis.

11. **What did you learn from this first web business?**

    From my first business, I learnt that it is not easy to make money online as I'd heard people saying before.

12. **What web businesses do you run now?**

    Despite of running my first web translations business, I'm also doing other freelance web marketing like online market research, link building, article writing, SEO etc.

13. **When did you start this?**

    I've started this on Feb 2005

14. **How much time did you devote to setting this up and running it?**

    For the first 5 months, only took about 3 hours daily to set up and running the services - build skills, literature review, market analysis, get clients etc.

15. **How much did it cost to set up and run?**

    There's no setup fees or cost for this because I'm just joining the freelancers' groups or websites to promo and get quoted.

16. **How much money do you make?**

    I've gain double as I got from my first business.

17. **What were the biggest challenges in setting up and running this web business?**

    Similar with my first web business.

18. **What are your top 5 goals for this web business?**

    My goals are:
    1. Double up the income every 3 months of sales.
    2. Open an online consultation agency for web business within a year.
    3. Can meet client satisfactions at competitive price.
    4. Expand the business to global markets.
    5. To be a professional web marketer or outsourcer in 2 years ahead.

19. **What top 5 tips would you give to somebody starting a business on line?**

    5 tips are :
    1. You need to understand the web business and have plenty of web experience to create successful business web sites.

2. In order to make a meaningful business web site, you have to make sure that you have an appealing home page that is easy to navigate; fresh and relevant content that will keep your visitors interested and answer frequently asked questions, offer something unique that will keep your visitors coming back to your business web site for more, and optimize the site for the search engines so the search engines rank it high on their index listings.

3. For beginner, Using a complete web site building solution can help you make the right business web site quickly, easily and at a reasonable price.

4. Creating a business web site doesn't have to be overly complicated, just choose a web development solution that makes sense for your business goals, resources, and customers.

5. Create goals that will lead you forward to the development of your business. Will your goal be traffic generation, sales, or other?

20. Do you plan to start any more web businesses in the next 24 months? If so, what are the details?

For the next 24 months, I'm planning to do online printing business i.e. business card, flyers, brochures etc.

21. What top 10 products or services would you recommend to somebody starting out online?

link building, SEO, translations, proofreading, copywriting, online printing, templates design, web designs, online bookstore and online market research.

22. Do you have any role models or mentors? If so, who are they, and how did you get them?

I do have severals mentors who guide me to this web business world, some of them are my clients which I knew them in the freelancers website. My role model is my brother who is a successful internet marketer.

23. What are you top 3 favourite reasons for running an online business?

I enjoy doing internet business because it has flexible working hours (which I can look after my babies), be the boss of my own business and can earn more than my salary before.

24. Any final words?

Setting web business goals is a great way to keep your focus on the direction you want your web business to take. Just make sure your web business goals are realistic and done in small increments. Also, review your web business goals regularly, and revise them to make sure they still fit with your web business direction.

You won't regret once you have join the world of web businesses.

www.malaylingua.com

■ **Stephen Luc   www.KeywordNichePower.com**

1. What was your first web business?

During my first two years I started with Ebay, and did a lot of affiliate marketing which meant I told other people's products for a commission. I made some good money then, but I'd have to say that my first extremely successful software product was called CB-NicheBuilder, located at CBNicheBuilder.com. It was a piece of software that allowed Clickbank Affiliate Marketers to find highly profitable products and build niche websites within a few minutes.

2. When did you start this?

I started this in July 2005, but it was pre-released in December 2005 and officially released in March 2006 where it then took off.

3. How much time did you devote to setting this up and running it?

During '05 I was working a full time day job, so I was spending time on the side to do my other businesses, but I spent about 3-4 hours a day finalizing this product.

During that time, I setup my system to take orders and automate distribution so most of my time was spent answering customer questions or problems. So for about 4 months I spent at least 6+ hours each night on the business. It was hard work, but it was very nice too.

4. How much did it cost to set up and run?

Domain and web hosting costs are always very little. You can a domain for about $8 a year and hosting for $25 per month. Web Design creation costs ran about $200 and product creation cost about $1500 at that time and about $2000 as the years passed. When running an Internet business, there is really no overhead costs, so you aren't losing money as the days go by. In fact, if you set up your business to be fully automated, the only staffing costs are when you run it. So a little under $4000 on investment.

5. How much money did you make?

Once it took off, I sold 1200 copies within a few months, which was promoted by some of the top Internet Marketers in the industry. It grossed well over $100K because it was a hot software product, but I used several JV Brokers and hundreds of affiliates, so I got about 30% of that amount. Not too bad for a few months release though and the experience that comes along with it.

6. What were the biggest challenges in setting up and running this web business?

The first two years I did Internet business were mostly failures because

I tried to do a lot of things on my own. That was a no no. I learned to seek guidance from an expert or mentor. So, I had advice from a mentor to set up everything correctly. Another big challenge is when you hit 75% of your project, that's the easy part, but finishing the remaining 25% to ensure everything is ready to go is the hard part.

While running the business, finding ways to market your product can be a tough because that is what defines whether or not you can make income or not. So it's important to know how to drive targeted traffic to a product site.

In fact most people tend to build a product and don't know how to market it. Online marketing is very different from Offline local marketing.

7. **What happened to the web business?**

   In 2008, I sold resell rights to my product to my customers so that they could profit from it. I have since then moved onto different business projects.

8. **Please provide any URLs / screenshots or other promo literature (sales page etc.)**

   http://www.CBNicheBuilder.com

9. **What is your background?**

   I majored in Computer Information Systems. As for business, I've always been the type of person who likes to find ways to sell stuff. I never had a business degree however.

10. **Did your background help with this web business in anyway?**

    My computer background helped when I produce the software. The Internet business background was self learned, but at that time I knew enough to get around. I've studied and been in Internet Marketing for 5 years as of 2008, so I've done everything from product development to web marketing consultation. So I can yes, it helped greatly.

11. **What did you learn from this first web business?**

    Plan ahead, including how you will produce the product, how you will set it up, and how you will promote it, all beforehand. Do your research. Not everyone will know how to setup a site to take payments and distribute things automatically, that is why research is very important or find an ebook or video that teaches this. Once you know how to do all these basics, then when you put all the pieces together you save time and you save money.

12. **What web businesses do you run now?**

    Since the launch of CBNicheBuilder, I released other software like KeywordNichePower.com that is being sold by thousands of resellers. I currently produce a lot of video training tutorials to teach newbies to advanced marketers about Internet Marketing at my site www.Instant-

PrivateLabelVideos.com. I spent much of 2007 producing many power ful softwares, so I'll be releasing those in 2008.

13. **When did you start this?**

I started www.InstantPrivateLabelVideos.com officially in August 2007.

14. **How much time did you devote to setting this up and running it?**

When I set this site up, it took about three months, a few hours per day Most of the time was spent on the sales copy to ensure that customers knew what they were buying and of course creating a solid video prod uct.

To run it, I spend about 3 hours a day to answer customer questions. I takes me about a week to produce the videos to ensure they are of qual ity each month.

15. **How much did it cost to set up and run?**

Most of this product was time spent on it. So total cost was less than $500 total.

16. **How much money do you make?**

With this site, I was making about the same as my 30 hour day job.

17. **What were the biggest challenges in setting up and running this web business?**

Getting everything situated and ready to go. To keep it running, to create videos, design graphics, and write sales letters each month was the most time consuming part. When I run it now, I spend most of my time marketing it and it's allowed me to focus on other projects and life.

18. **What are your top 5 goals for this web business?**

- Help educate business owners about using Internet Marketing.
- Help my customers succeed by advising them in the training center.
- Constantly bringing in some top notch quality videos that customers can sell and profit from.
- Use it as a platform to build more video products.
- Turn newbies into advanced marketers.

19. **What top 5 tips would you give to somebody starting a business online?**

- Do not jump on every how to make money product out there, otherwise you will overwhelm yourself and give up. Find one, stick with it, implement it, study it, research it, otherwise you will be like many who just buy everything but don't make money. The best way is to purchase a product where you know you can easily reach the product owner.
- Do not try to do everything on your own, meaning learn from other expert's mistakes. Seek guidance from an expert in your field and follow them. Find experts who focus on helping newbies and advanced

marketers succeed.

- Network and build relationships. Surround yourself with like minded people, because when the times get rough, you can turn to them for support. Places like the warriorforum.com/forum is a good place to start.
- Learn from your failures so that you can constantly tweak your business plans to success. Focus on automation so you can spend less time on certain areas of your business and more time on what needs to be done.
- Don't forget to build your list, this one is a big one. If you don't know how, read about it because it's one of the most important things in Internet business.

20. Do you plan to start any more web businesses in the next 24 months? If so, what are the details?

Yes, of course. In fact I create many web businesses continually, even now. There is no reason for stopping. As you saw in my earlier examples, web businesses produce little overhead costs, so you can produce many. If you go into something like ebooks, you could spend even less than $50 to get started.

However the key is to only produce more when your other ones are doing well. Don't keep jumping onto new ideas.

Most of my products are geared towards helping Internet businesses grow, so it will most likely be a piece of software that speeds things up to save time or videos that teach.

21. What top 10 products or services would you recommend to somebody starting out online?

- Get on the WarriorForum.com/Forum , the best place of people to go to get Internet Marketing help. That's where I started years ago, and it's helped me not only to network, to find like minded people.
- Aweber.com – To start a list, I'd highly recommend that you use a 3rd party autoresponder service so that you can start building your lists.
- Namecheap.com – Great and cheap place to get your domain names.
- WebHostingTalk.com – Great forum where you can find rock bottom web hosting deals for your website's web hosting needs.
- Scriptlance.com – Great place to find programmers to fill your software development or script installation needs.
- RentACoder.com – Great place to outsource your business needs in case your business grows and you need people to do things so you can focus on other things.
- NVU Web Editor Tool – Great web editor tool for newbies that know

nothing about HTML or Web programming code. Building a basic page is a big necessity for website owners.

- DLGuard or Amember Pro – Great web scripts that allow you to create a membership site or automated system to sell your products, ebooks, software, videos, etc. When you do online business, you need to have it so people can pay and instantly download your products, so you can focus on the most important things such as customer support, product creation, and marketing.

- E-Counter – You can google this software, but whenever you do certain tasks, you should put a time limit on yourself so that you can get things done. The worst thing about online business is that you can get easily distracted because you are connected to the Internet. What better way than to not only give yourself a time limit, but have it remind you when you are over the time limit.

- Clickbank.com – The biggest digital marketplace to find products as an affiliate marketer to sell. The commission rates are huge, generally anywhere from 50-75%. If you are not a member, then I suggest you go there to see what they offer and find ebooks or software on it. This was the first place I started making money and since then, it's been the best income thus far.

22. Do you have any role models or mentors? If so, who are they, and how did you get them?

Mentors:

Gary Durkin - A good friend I would consider a mentor from the Warrior Forum during my early times. Whenever I had questions about how to approach the business successfully, I would ask him for advice. Since then I have focused on helping others who started out like me without a mentor.

Michael Nicholas - First to promote my CBNicheBuilder product before it took off like crazy. From that point one, he gave me advice that I eventually would implement and do well with. Since then we've been great business friends.

23. What are you top 3 favourite reasons for running an online business? (E.g. flexible hours, run my own business, access to global markets etc.)

I like it because of the global reach. I can help business people all around the world succeed; not just in one set location. Flexible hours is another great thing now that I quit my job. I can do the business when I want. But I really have to be motivated.

24. Any final words?

I'm sure you've all heard that you can money online 24/7 even while you're sleeping. While that may be true, I honestly will say that it is a business, so it is a lot of hard work to setup and run a business. Once you reach the point of moving it along, then that's the easy part. In Internet business you really have to be motivated and persistent to reach your goal.

Sometimes you go months without making a dime in the beginning, but if you persevere and don't let tiny roadblocks stop you, then you can do well. If you can keep moving even when times are rough, that is a test of how well you will do. Just remember, everything is a two way street, seek help, but also give it to those that need it, build relationships in your industry, and you will do well. Keep your head up high and don't allow things to stop you.

Michael Fleischner   http://marketing-expert.blogspot.com

1. What was your first web business?

My first web business was selling affiliate based products online, earning commissions with each sale. This was really the way that I leveraged my first website, http://www.marketingscoop.com which was really just developed to provide free information and resources to marketers.

The site still exists today and continues to generate a constant stream of visitors and revenue.

2. When did you start this?

The site launched in February of 2004, but I was planning and working on the site for about ten months prior to launch.

3. How much time did you devote to setting this up and running it?

Most of my time was spent on developing the site, adding content on a regular basis, and marketing the site.

For me, traffic was everything and I spent the majority of my time on SEO and site usability - probably between 2 and 3 hours/day. The site also took a lot of work to initially set up and I was spending the same, about 2 - 3 hours on it each day, adding content and programming HTML.

In addition to spending on average about three hours a day on SEO, I did spend a couple of hours each day reviewing affiliate products, speaking with potential partners, and responding to prospect inquiries.

4. How much did it cost to set up and run?

The first site took some time to develop. And because I was starting out, I didn't have a lot of money to spend. I think when all was said and done, it cost about $15K - $18K to get the site developed, marketed, and maintained.

5. How much money did you make?

The first year I didn't make much, maybe $1K- $2K. By the third year was making between $3K - $4K per month. This was a direct result of the increase in traffic I developed over that 2 - 3 year period.

6. **What were the biggest challenges in setting up and running this web business?**

The biggest challenge was the realization that I "didn't having a clue" when it came to starting my own business.

When I started out, no one gave me a clear roadmap to follow (i.e. do this, don't do this). As a result, I got many things wrong and had to redo them. This cost me time and money and could have been avoided if a roadmap was provided.

7. **What happened to the web business?**

I still own the web business, but it's essentially on autopilot. Because the site is so well established, most of the content comes from loyal users who submit valuable resources.

In addition, I'm not longer looking for great affiliate products, they come to me. By having a strong performing site that requires only a small bit of maintenance, I can focus on other endeavors while providing value to MarketingScoop.com loyalists who still value all of the free marketing resources and information the site provides.

8. **Please provide any URLs / screenshots or other promo literature (sales page etc.)**

http://www.marketingscoop.com (ranked #1 for 'marketing expert' 'free marketing articles', and top 3 on Google for 'marketing articles')

9. **What is your background? (education, hobbies etc.).**

My background is in Marketing. I attended Rutgers College for Undergrad and received my Graduate degree from Northwestern University in Integrated Marketing Communications. My formal education taught me that you always need to keep the big picture in mind while learning how to manage the specific objectives needed to be successful. I've also had about 3 very powerful mentors in my life and I think this has really shaped my success.

10. **Did your background help with this web business in anyway?**

These experiences definitely shaped my online businesses and continue to serve me today. One of the most important lessons I learned is that nothing is impossible. What's capable online is a true testiment to that statement. If you have an idea, the web can help you make it a reality. I also learned that to succeed online you need to put yourself in the browsers shoes and segment your market.

This is so important today and something that many of the clients for whom I consult, just plain miss.

11. What did you learn from this first web business?

Businesses don't run on their own. Yes, over time, your business builds a base and its much easier to operate, but it takes constant vigilance.

12. What web businesses fo you run now?

I run a couple of blogs (The Marketing Blog (http://marketing-expert.blogspot.com), The Good markeitng Tips Blog (http://goodmarketingtips.blogspot.com)), and have created one of the Internet's most popular ebooks on Search Engine Optimization at http://www.webmastersbookofsecrets.com in addition to my original and primary website, MarketingScoop.com.

13. When did you start this?

I started developing these other websites and blogs in 2006.

14. How much time did you devote to setting this up and running it?

I spent a good deal of time working on many of these projects simultaneously. I would say that I spent on average 6- 8 hours per day, six days per week.

15. How much did it cost to set up and run?

My blogs were virtually free. My websites, MarketingScoop.com and WebmastersBookofSecrets cost about $18K and $4K respectively. Combined, I think the total investment was about $25K with the largest expense being design and programming.

16. How much money do you make?

Today, my income from my online properties generates the same as my full-time salary. That's a great cushion in case I ever want to leave my day job as a full-time marketing executive.

17. What were the biggest challenges in setting up and running this web business?

Keeping up with it all. Sometimes you don't have enough time to focus on what's most important - your customers. Over time it does get easier to manage multiple tasks, but there are so many additional things I would like to do if only I had more time and resources.

18. What are your top 5 goals for this web business?

To increase site revenue per customer, to improve search rankings for select keywords, to build a larger base of prospective customers, improve Alexa ranking, to be purchased by another website or company that is strategically aligned with the business.

19. What top 5 tips would you give to somebody starting a business online?

All it takes is a great idea and persistence to see that dream become a reality. If you have an idea, than get started, don't delay. There is plenty of free advice online on how to start and grow your very own online business.

20. **Do you plan to start any more web businesses in the next 24 months. If so, what are the details?**

The only other project I have going on right now is the publishing of my first book for trade distribution (B & N, Borders, Amazon.com) entitled, "SEO Made Simple: Strategies for Dominating the World's Largest Search Engine." The book will be launched in April of this year (2008) and can help anyone doing business online improve their search engine rankings on Google - the world's largest search engine. To support the book and offer readers a bonus, I'm creating a new website called myseomadesimple.com.

21. **What top 10 products or services would you recommend to somebody starting out online?**

I suggest the following: "The Webmasters Book of Secrets", "SEO Elite" "Directory Submitter Pro", "Article Submitter Pro", "Good Keywords" and "MailChimp" This will take care of almost everything you need to grow your web business.

Also, for cheap domains use GoDaddy.com.

22. **Do you have any role models or mentors? If so, who are they, and how did you get them?**

My online role model is Brad Callen. He's created some tremendous online products and is a real pioneer in online marketing.

23. **What are you top 3 favourite reasons for running an online business?**

Fun, Fun, and Fun. Running your own online business is very enjoyable. The flexibility is great too. You can work on it whenever, whereever you choose.

24. **Any final words? Think big.**

The Marketing Blog: http://marketing-expert.blogspot.com

Good Marketing Tips: http://goodmarketingtips.blogspot.com

MarketingScoop: http://www.marketingscoop.com

Webmasters Book of Secrets: http://www.webmastersbookofsecrets. com

My SEO Made Simple (coming soon): http://myseomadesimple.com

■ **Leslie Householder www.ThoughtsAlive.com**

1. What was your first web business?

www.ThoughtsAlive.com for teaching principles of success

2. When did you start this?

October 2002

3. How much time did you devote to setting this up and running it?

To understand how this all happened I need to offer a little bit of history: I had recently started teaching seminars on the laws of success among just friends and family. I pictured myself becoming a world-class seminar speaker, but at the time it was just a dream.

Simultaneously, something occurred that turned my life upside down. I was consumed with anger toward an individual, someone I felt had stabbed me in the back, and my bitterness was negatively affecting my business and family life. I knew I had to do something to just let it go and move on. After exhausting all other resources I could think of to help me heal, I reluctantly turned to the internet... a place of the "dangerous unknown." Immediately I found SheLovesGod.com, became a subscriber, and in time, the owner sent an article on forgiveness. It didn't change how I felt inside, but it caused me to reply and ask for her perspective on my dilemma. It didn't take long before she expressed her personal frustration with money issues, and I replied, "Money problems? I can help you with that!"

So over the phone and through email and text messaging, I took her informally through the material in my seminars, and in the next month she doubled her internet sales from $2000 to $4000. The month after that she doubled it again to $8000.

She was so excited about what she had learned that she asked me to write a series of articles for her subscribers on the seven laws. About six months later she asked me to be a guest presenter at her virtual women's conference.

However, about a week before the conference, she realized that the listeners would need a place to go to learn more about me after the call. "You need a website!!" she exclaimed.

So she showed me how to set up a very basic page within a week via telephone and instant messaging. Of course it was probably 10-16 hours a day because I had a very steep learning curve. I simply took a copy of one of her webpages and edited the text to suit me.

4. **How much did it cost to set up and run?**

It wasn't very expensive at all. The scary part wasn't so much spending the money, it was committing to a monthly hosting fee and wondering if the investment was ever going to come back to me. I had seen the principles or laws of success work wonders for us in helping my husband get a better job, and helping us begin to be successful real estate investors, but I was brand new at teaching seminars and internet marketing. I had yet to prove the principles in THESE new endeavors.

I believe my initial costs back in 2002 consisted of my domain name ($10) and a hosting service (I can't remember, maybe $6-10/month).

My friend let me have access to her list management service and created an autoresponder within it for MY list which I used for about a year, until I felt like I needed to wean myself from her help. I obtained my own account with smartautoresponder.com because it was simple and easy to use. I believe it cost me about $70 for a year's service. I've since moved to the 1shoppingcart.com system because it integrates the list managment service with my shopping cart and the paypal merchant services, and now together costs me closer to $150/mo.

As for the initial content of my website, my friend copied the code from one of her sites and put it on my empty domain. Then she showed me how to edit the text and upload my own pictures using a free trial version of EditPlus and a free FTP uploader program called FileZilla from SourceForge.net.

I began paying for subscribers through a list builder service, $60 here and there, until my list size was about 1000. Then I stopped buying leads, intending to wait until I had a handful of things to sell them.

Everything I offered for the first 2 1/2 years was digital, so there was very little capital outlay for product creation... just time. I wrote articles, submitted them to shelovesgod.com for storage (no charge) and in time gathered them together and created a PDF ebook out of them, using Clickbank to sell it. I designed my own graphics with $50 in images from Corbis.com and using Microsoft Paint. It cost me $50 to set up the account with Clickbank, and for several years, my friend converted my Word files to PDF for me because I didn't know how to do them myself. Now I convert them with one of the many free PDF creator programs.

There was no such thing as "balance" to how I juggled life back then. Laundry piled up, meals were thrown together at the last minute or forgotten completely. Sometimes I worked more than 14 hours a day, tending to the family only when absolutely necessary. I was driven by the dream of creating something passive, so I could enjoy my family full time and not leave home for a job, and lay a foundation for a prosperous future. I set my business goals according to what I wanted to have in place by the time the oldest was a teenager. In the meantime, the kids played on the floor near my computer making messes that remained for weeks at a time.

5. **How much money did you make?**
   Next to nothing. Maybe $5 here or there.

6. **What were the biggest challenges in setting up and running this web business?**
   Even though I had taught a few traditional seminars, teaching that first

class over the phone for my friend was terrifying. It was so strange to speak to a group of people that I couldn't see. I was used to getting visual feedback from my audiences, so this was tough to remain energetic with nothing more than an imagined audience of excited people. I think there were only about 3 people on the call, but getting through it was a milestone for me.

But even harder than that was learning html by trial and error, juggling a household of (at the time) four little kids, pregnant with number five, moving to a two-bedroom fixer-upper investment property with broken air conditioning, living among black widow spiders and bare tackstrip where all the carpets had been pulled up, all with my husband working a job 2 1/2 hours away. We'd work on rennovations on the weekends and I'd work on my writing projects and the web business during the week.

I didn't find out until about 4 or 5 years later that there are wysiwyg programs to help you build sites without knowledge of code. However, even if I HAD known about them, I probably wouldn't have invested in one because I enjoyed deleting pieces of code to find out what it would do to a page, and I got a charge out of finding ways to do what needed to be done on a shoestring budget. Tables, columns and rows brought me the most grief. Remove one tiny little <tr> tag and your entire page looks like something exploded on it.

My husband still rolls his eyes when I forget to close my tags (every <tr> should also have a </tr>, and so forth). Hey, I figure if it doesn't mess up the page to have it missing, why must I bother?

I've since learned to use some javascript and php as well. I don't understand it, but I've found you don't have to understand something in order to use it. Eventually I invested in a program by Vertical Moon called SWF n Slide to create my Jackrabbit Factor 4-minute movie at www.jackrabbitfactor.com which has helped with some viral marketing.

7. **What happened to the web business?**

I still own it. In 2005 I spent $600 on a cover design, $70 on an account with a Print-on-Demand book printer (LightningSource.com) and self-published "The Jackrabbit Factor: Why You Can." Then I used an internet marketing campaign to launch it. I had typset it myself in Microsoft Word (many tears later - realized the key to typesetting is in using a "gutter") and with endorsements from Stephen Covey (7 Habits of Highly Effective People) and Bob Procor (from The Secret - before it came out) it became a #5 national bestseller for a whole 6 hours, outranking even the new Harry Potter at the time (which impressed my kids at the very least).

My other book, "Hidden Treasures: Heaven's Astonishing Help with

Your Money Matters" (which began as that original collection of articles for my friend's subscribers at shelovesgod.com in 2002) organically became an Amazon Bestseller in September 2007 (even without big name endorsers, and without an internet campaign) ...and at the time I write this, has continued to show up regularly in the Money and Values top 100 - six months and counting.

In 2006 after moving from the fixer upper, we took equity from our home and invested several thousand dollars in a Marketing Coach: Charlie Cook. At that time (4 years after its inception) I was only making about $30/month passive income through the website. After implementing his strategies, my site began to generate $4000/month. By this time my husband had already left his job to be an investor and learn the financial services industry, but in the fall of 2007 decided to set aside his other interests to help me build the web business full time. He closes my html tags and thanks to his vision for the business (which tends to be much bigger than mine) we have been able to do more faster than ever. One of the first projects he undertook was to add a forum to our site which has been a huge value-add for our visitors.

The site has grown and developed into a full blown community for others seeking to understand and implement the fundamental principles of prosperity. We now publish physical books, have a forum, a blog, a bookstore, an affiliate program, an article library, mentorship programs, ecourses, seminars, and avenues for promoting others who have products or services to help families achieve prosperity. The site has provided us with a six-figure income for the last two years and the revenue continues to grow. It was a happy day when our CPA announced that we had officially turned a profit, five years after the site was born. Presently, it is staffed by me and my husband only, but we are extremely busy (with seven children under sixteen years old besides) and foresee the need to expand our work force. We have hired contractors along the way to help us with aspects of the technology we didn't understand, totalling about $10,000.

8. **Please provide any URLs / screenshots or other promo literature (sales page etc.)**

   http://www.thoughtsalive.com - free 19 Rules of Prosperity Guide

   http://www.jackrabbitfactor.com - free 4-minute movie and download of Jackrabbit Factor ebook

   http://www.thoughtsalive.com/prosperyourfamily.php - 8 week Jackrabbit Factor ecourse

   http://www.prosperyourfamily.com - 12 week Family Time & Money Freedom Home Study Course

9. What is your background? (education, hobbies etc.)

I am a wife and mother of seven children ages 1-15. I graduated from Brigham Young University in Mathematics Education and taught junior high math part time for about 3 years. I love to read. I enjoy movies that motivate and inspire. In 2001 I trained with Bob Proctor's company to facilitate his seminars, years before he appeared on "The Secret." I am a contributing author to multiple Chicken Soup for the Soul publications.

10. Did your background help with this web business in anyway?

Indirectly... My mathematics background helped me with problem solving and believing that there is always a solution. No matter what problem comes my way, I know there is a solution and I have learned how to enlist and trust my subconscious mind/inspiration to help me discover it. In my days at college when I'd stare at a problem for hours and try to force the answer, I learned to do my best and then forget about it for a while. The answer would often show up in my mind when I was in the twilight zone between sleep and being awake. I learned to write it down immediately so that I could see if it truly did still make sense in the morning. I still approach problems that way, and that has helped me keep going in the business even when it seemed like there was no way around the obstacles we've faced along the way.

11. What did you learn from this first web business?

I learned the importance of building a database. Your subscriber list is your gold mine. I also learned the importance of investing in good marketing advice. I would much rather have an ugly website that has a good conversion rate than a pretty one that makes nothing. If funds are limited, spend the money on learning marketing strategies and make it pretty later. Also, people want free content that is valuable and helps them get what they want. Give enough good stuff for free and you'll develop a relationship of trust so that they will have confidence in purchasing your products later. Supply good customer service and create raving fans. Even if you can't be found on the search engines, you can utilize the power of word-of-mouth advertising if people are pleased and amazed by how you treat them.

12. What web businesses do you run now?

I still run ThoughtsAlive.com. But now we also have www.jackrabbit-factor.com, www.hiddentreasuresbook.com, www.successassured.com, www.prosperyourfamily.com, and countless others on the horizon. Every time we get a great idea, we go buy a domain name for it. It may take years to create them all, but it's a process we have grown to love.

13. When did you start this?

Our first (www.thoughtsalive.com) was started in October 2002 We created www.jackrabbitfactor.com in 2005, and our most recent (in development) is www.successassured.com.

14. **How much time did you devote to setting this up and running it?**

Honestly, we love what we do so much we spend every moment we can building our websites. The best part is having the freedom to do it or not as we please. We've recently been spending maybe 6 hours a day responding to customer enquires, but have just developed some new systems to handle most of them automatically. This will probably cut the time required in half. Soon, we expect to hire a virtual assistant to handle the day-to-day support (or train one of our kids) and enlist a fulfilment house to handle orders.

15. **How much did it cost to set up and run?**

ThoughtsAlive.com is still our primary business, so please refer to answers already listed above.

16. **How much money do you make?**

The most I've ever made at a job was $6000/year. My web business has generated six figures for the last two years and is climbing, while work time it requires is diminishing.

17. **What were the biggest challenges in setting up and running this web business?**

see above

18. **What are your top 5 goals for this web business?**

*   Reach 2 million Jackrabbit Factor readers
*   Be the #1 Prosperity website on the internet
*   Develop the ThoughtsAlive Mentor Directory to feature 1000 Mentors who understand and use "Jackrabbit Speak"
*   Gather a qualified team of ThoughtsAlive Official Mentors and ThoughtsAlive Coaches to service the 2 million JF readers.
*   See the Jackrabbit Factor story become a theater-based major motion picture blockbuster.
    (a sixth goal: Have everything we offer at ThoughtsAlive.com translated into Spanish.)

19. **What top 5 tips would you give to somebody starting a business online?**

1. Begin by writing articles and just getting what's in your head online.
2. The easiest way to get started is with a blog - and you can set one up for free. No need to understand code, no hosting, etc.
3. Start building a list of subscribers
4. Don't wait for everything to be perfect
5. Don't be afraid to invest in good help - the kind that will help you

generate revenue. Web design is secondary. There are a lot of ugly websites that make a lot of money, and a lot of pretty ones that are strapped because they spent too much money on set-up and design. Decide what you'd rather have: money or looks?

20. Do you plan to start any more web businesses in the next 24 months? If so, what are the details?

Are you kidding? We can't stop thinking of ideas. One of them is to create an online swap meet for kids. Last month my 9 year-old daughter created some Valentine's gift bags and asked me to announce them to my list. In less than a week she generated $160. To thank the people on my list who supported her entrepreneurial spirit, I want to create a system where the children of THOSE customers can sell something THEY created. If a parent wants their child's creation at the swap meet, all they have to do is first buy something at the swap meet to support someone else's kid first... and so on.

21. What top 10 products or services would you recommend to somebody starting out online?

www.blogger.com - start a blog

www.istockphoto.com - stock photography for as little as $1 per image

www.marketerschoice.com - shopping cart, database management, autoresponders, affiliate program management (uses the 1shoppingcart system with a better user interface, in my opinion)

www.paypal.com - payment gateway and virtual terminal

www.sourceforge.net for PDFcreator (create ebooks) and FileZilla (FTP uploading)

www.editplus.com - if you want to learn code by trial and error like I did

www.snagit.com (more powerful than Microsoft Paint, easier to learn than Photoshop)

www.lightningsource.com - the best and cheapest in Print on Demand book publishing

www.godaddy.com - domain purchasing

www.marketingforsuccess.com - great marketing tips, fantastic newsletter

22. Do you have any role models or mentors? If so, who are they, and how did you get them?

(Each one has a long story behind how I got them... so in a nutshell, when I (the student) was ready, the teacher appeared.)

Bob Proctor - success psychology

Charlie Cook - marketing

Randy Gilbert - book promotion

Yanik Silver - marketing

Marnie Pehrson - site development, marketing

23. What are your top 3 favourite reasons for running an online business?

Flexible hours. Reach people and affect lives all over the world. Don't have to wear heels.

24. Any final words?

Just make that decision of what kind of lifestyle you want for your family, and trust that the right idea will come to you at the right time. Honor the ideas when they come, nurture them like a new baby, and give them time to grow. You don't have to know or have everything you'll need right now. You already have everything you need to get started, and that's all that matters. Your web business grows and develops each time you put something new in it. The only thing that would prevent it from growing is if you stop, and the only thing that reverses the process is if you start deleting. Each day add something to it, and one day you'll look back and be amazed at what you've accomplished!

http://www.thoughtsalive.com

- ■ **Nicole Dean   http://www.NicoleOntheNet.com**

  1. What was your first web business?

  My first website was www.ShowMomtheMoney.com -- I created this website to showcase work from home ideas, business, and opportunities, as well as provide tips for moms to stay "mostly-sane" while working from home.

  2. When did you start this?

  June 10, 2004

  3. How much time did you devote to setting this up and running it?

  Initially I spent a lot of time, researching, learning html, studying search engine optimization, networking with others, etc. It became my passion and my "life" as our family finances at the time made it imperative that I work hard and make money quickly. So, I probably worked 8 or more hours per day, 7 days each week. Now, I spend only a few hours each month on this website.

  4. How much did it cost to set up and run?

  Domain registration through GoDaddy. $8

  Hosting $5/month

  Autoresponder $17/month

  5. How much money did you make?

  Initially it was only about $100 or so per month. Of course, that has grown since then.

6. **What were the biggest challenges in setting up and running this web business?**

I always tell people that I clawed my way up the learning curve. I'm not technical at all, so learning to build websites was very stressful. I'd break stuff constantly and have to have my husband fix it while I stressed out. I still don't know how to do graphics, I outsource it. I hire out other tasks that I don't have the time or inclination to learn. Thank goodness for outsourcing. It's my best friend.

7. **What happened to the web business?**

I still own this website.

8. **Please provide any URLs / screenshots or other promo literature (sales page etc.)**

www.ShowMomtheMoney.com

9. **What is your background? (education, hobbies etc.)**

My degree is in Psychology. After college, I worked for a bank in purchasing and then documentation after that. I was the one who wrote bank manuals. Let's just say that it gave me the skills to write under pressure. My hobbies are belly dancing, roller blading, hiking, biking, canoeing, and reading. Of course, working on my business is also my most enjoyable thing to do with my time now.

10. **Did your background help with this web business in anyway ?**

Studying Psychology has helped me in all areas of my life. It enables me to see past what people say and do and understand them better. This certainly helps me in working with others as well. It also helps me to be a better parent. (I hope.)

Writing for the bank definitely helped me with my writing skills. Learning how to explain complex procedures so that an 18 year old teller could pick up the book and follow the steps -- that helped me in countless ways writing ebooks and tutorials in my business.

11. **What did you learn from this first web business?**

I learned html and a lot of patience. I learned how to network and market a business. Most importantly I learned confidence.

12. **What web businesses do you run now?**

I wear several different hats now. I write and sell my own ebooks to help moms work from home. I create information websites that are free for others to read. I work as a consultant helping others market their websites. And, I sell private label articles and reports (PLR) for web owners. PLR articles are written by professionals and the web or blog owners can buy them and use them on their own websites, blogs, or in their ezines. (You can see a better example of what I mean at www.EasyPLR.com).

13. **When did you start this?**

My business has been an ongoing progression. I'm always adding new projects and adapting things to work better.

14. How much time did you devote to setting this up and running it?

I'll answer this question in regards to consulting. I spend approximately 20 hours/week. Sometimes it will be as much as 100 hours. Other times it's 5 hours. It depends on the needs of my clients at the time.

15. How much did it cost to set up and run?

This business (consulting) costs the same as any other to set up. Domain $8. Hosting $5/month. The biggest expense for me is paying my helpers. Thank God for them! I hire work at home moms. (Something I'm very proud of.) I pay them between $8 and $25 per hour depending on their skill set.

16. How much money do you make?

I make more (after expenses) than I did working at the bank, and more than my husband does. ;) I'm very private about money, so I hope that's a good enough answer.

17. What were the biggest challenges in setting up and running this web business?

Again, it was probably confidence. The internet marketing world is highly competitive and I have to remind myself on a daily basis that I know more than 99.9% of the population of the world does about this topic. It's hard, though, at times, when I'm entrenched in this field with so many others who are in the business to realize that we are still the minority and many people will pay (and pay well) for our expertise.

18. What are your top 5 goals for this web business?

My goals are to be able to pay it forward and continue hiring my friends. I want to be able to pay out twice as much money this year to my helpers as I did last year. Every one of my helpers who I can help to stay home with their kids is another bright and shiny trophy on my shelf.

19. What top 5 tips would you give to somebody starting a business on line?

1. You can't make money from ideas. You must put them into action.
2. When you fall, get back up.
3. Pay it forward. It always comes back to you in spades.
4. Network with people smarter than you.
5. Hire help when you get stuck.
6. Look back so you can see your progress often. Even baby steps are moving you ahead.

20. Do you plan to start any more web businesses in the next 24 months? If so, what are the details?

Certainly. I always do. I plan to revamp some of my sites in the coming days. www.FreeAffiliateArticles.com is getting a face lift, for instance. I also plan to start a portal for my information products. Working as a consultant definitely slowed my progress on that, so I'm excited to get that up and running.

21. What top 10 products or services would you recommend to somebody starting out online?

1. MomWebs.com - my favorite web host. Great support.
2. Aweber.com - great autoresponder.
3. MomsMastermind.com - awesome place to network with other women.
4. WebTrafficBasics.com - my free course on getting more web traffic.
5. ListandTrafficNow.com - this site opened my mind. Great reports each month. Defintely "outside the box" thinking.
6. OneMinuteSurveys.com - allows you to poll your readers.
7. DineWithoutWhine.com - menu planner that helps you to be more efficient.
8. OutsourceSweetie.com - helps you start outsourcing effectively.
9. Clickbank.com - An easy way to sell your ebooks.
10. EasyPrivateLabelArticles.com - Another free course about using private label articles to save you time and money.

22. Do you have any role models or mentors? If so, who are they, and how did you get them?

My #1 mentor is Jimmy D. Brown who also happens to be a friend and client. (I'm his affiliate manager.) His website is 123WebMarketing.com -- he's definitely one of the good guys. If you're going to learn from anyone -- I'd recommend him.

23. What are you top 3 favourite reasons for running an online business?

It would be very difficult where I live to find a job that pays more than I make now and has any degree of flexibility. When the kids are sick, they stay home with me. When my mom had surgery earlier this year, I was able to take care of her without having to beg to a boss. That meant the world to me that I was able to be there for her as much as she needed me. It's about being able to make choices in my life based upon MY needs and not on what a boss feels is best for the company. I hope that I give my helpers the same sense of comfort. Now, I'm getting a little teary eyed. ;)

24. Any final words?

My blog is at http://www.NicoleOnTheNet.com -- I share a lot of awesome freebies there as well as great content. And, I throw in some silliness at times, as well.

My final words are to just do it. If it's too overwhelming, there are op-

tions. Decide which path you're going to follow and follow it. For in
stance, if you're going to blog, then buy a domain name, buy hosting
and find someone to install Word Press for you. Start writing and learr
as you go. Researching for another year just means you'll have to wai
another year to see any profits. I wish you the best.

Warmly,

Nicole Dean

- **Kevin Riley   http://productcreationlabs.com**
  1. **What was your first web business?**

     The concept of Autonet was to work with Vancouver
     Island car dealerships and help them move their used
     cars. We got a programmer to create a searchable da-
     tabase where prospects could enter info about the
     kind of car they were looking for (Make, model, year
     range, price range) and the database would find what
     was available.

     We didn't have a digital camera -- or even know about digital cameras
     yet. My partner was taking Polaroid photos, I was scanning them in with
     a ScanMan, and uploading the pics and data to our database.

     My partner was out visiting dealerships to sell our service.
  2. **When did you start this?**

     1995
  3. **How much time did you devote to setting this up and running it?**

     I was spending a few hours a week entering vehicles (We never go
     more than one dealership to sign up). Then, I was also spending quite a
     few hours a week writing content to bring in visitors. Articles about car
     maintenance, buying used cars, etc.
  4. **How much did it cost to set up and run?**

     In those days, we got our domain through our provider. Setting up the
     domain cost us $800. Getting the database created was about $1500.
     We also spent about $100 getting photos of our webpages printed up
     so we could show them to our prospective dealerships. The logo -- a
     cartoon car going around a globe -- I created in Corel Draw.
  5. **How much money did you make?**

     Very little. We gave a massive discount to get that one dealership to try
     it out.
  6. **What were the biggest challenges in setting up and running this web
     business?**

     The fact that none of the car dealers even knew what Internet was. They
     had no connection, so we had to provide photos of our website and

explain Internet to them. Basically, we were too far ahead of the curve.

7. What happened to the web business?

Closed it about a half year later.

8. Please provide any URLs / screenshots or other promo literature (sales page etc.)

That was so long ago, you can't even find it in the archives of the Wayback Machine.

9. What is your background? (education, hobbies etc.)

I grew up in Klosters, Switzerland and my family emigrated to Canada in the late 60s. I started building businesses as soon as I started college. Most were in small manufacturing, as I have always loved creating things. I had a candle factory, wooden toy kits factory, board game company, among other ventures.

I went on to become a mechanical engineer, which I never used much but the knowledge came in handy in my house building company.

10. Did your background help with this web business in anyway ?

Yes, it did. Being creative and having some experience with assembling things, I found it easy to get the hang of HTML and was soon building websites, right after my first exposure to Internet in 1994.

11. What did you learn from this first web business?

I learned that you should sell what people are buying. If you try to introduce prospects to something new, that they don't even know they want or need, it is a very hard thing to sell.

12. What web businesses do you run now?

I run Product Creation Labs from my home office in Osaka, Japan. I sell information products all over the world. These are e-books and videos to help people get started creating their own information products (or how-to books) in many different niches, and market them online.

13. When did you start this?

I started the Product Creation Labs with my "Mission: Make Money Online" video home study course in Oct 2006.

14. How much time did you devote to setting this up and running it?

During start up, I was spending about 20-30 hours per week. Now, I have so many new project ideas that I am working full time on this business.

15. How much did it cost to set up and run?

Nowadays, domain registration is cheap. I have about 60-70 domain names (Not all in use), and they each cost me less than $20 for two years of registration. I spend about $300 per month on hosting. I also spend $20 per month on my autoresponder, which is the best $20 I spend each month -- it is such a valuable asset.

Product creation is done by me, but there were initial software costs -- like Camtasia screen capture video software for $300 and Snag It for $40. outsource my e-covers for about $20-30 each. Because I use outsourcing to take care of any tasks like graphics and article writing, I have no employees. There is also zero inventory, as all my products are digital.

16. **How much money do you make?**

I'll just say that I make enough for a comfortable living in the expensive city of Osaka, Japan. My wife an I love traveling and going out to good restaurants, and my business provides for that.

17. **What were the biggest challenges in setting up and running this web business?**

Staying organized and focused is the biggest challenge. It's way too easy to be distracted by all the opportunities, methods, and technology online.

18. **What are your top 5 goals for this web business?**

Create a good, solid line of products. Develop a good reputation with my market. Create a steady income that allows frequent world travel. Have a long-term business. Create a lot of happy customers. To be honest, I think I have fulfilled all my goals.

19. **What top 5 tips would you give to somebody starting a business online?**

Number one would have to be "Be persistent". Too many people start out on one idea, then lose focus, see another opportunity, and switch to it. Jumping from one idea to another is a surefire way to fail. I suggest that before you start your online business you sit back and give it a very hard thinking over. You want to get started building a business that you are going to be working with for a very long time.

Another thing to avoid is trying to be too unique. Do not try to sell people something they are not already buying. If someone is buying books on fly tying, it is because they have an interest in fly tying and they will buy more books on it.

At the same time, don't follow the crowd too closely. You want to bring out the same kind of product, but you don't want it to be the same. See what others are buying and improve on it. Make it easier to use, make it more fun, make it more effective.

Do something you really want to do. You need to have some passion for your business, as you'll be doing it for a long time and without passion you won't put in the energy required to make it really successful.

20. **Do you plan to start any more web businesses in the next 24 months? If so, what are the details?**

I plan on producing many more products for my existing web business.

but not more businesses. I don't recommend diluting marketing efforts with too many different businesses. I'd rather focus my efforts on creating my product line.

21. **What top 10 products or services would you recommend to somebody starting out online?**

It depends on what kind of online venture you decide to pursue, but if you want to create and market info products, there are some good basics to have: A good hosting service (an easy one for beginners, but robust, is Host4Profit), a reliable autoresponder service (Aweber), a good PDF editor (Open Office is free), Camtasia for creating screencapture and slideshow videos, SnagIt for screencapture photos, Warrior Forum for meeting other maketers, Skype for developing online relationships, an HTML editor (Nvu is free and easy to use), an FTP program for uploading your sites (I like CuteFTP), and an online e-mail service (like GMail) so you can check your e-mail from anywhere in the world.

22. **Do you have any role models or mentors? If so, who are they, and how did you get them?**

I am basically a student from the school of hard knocks. Although I attended a few business seminars in my early years (1970s and 80s), most of what I have learned has been from running my own businesses and studying. I study new methods all the time and love case studies.

23. **What are you top 3 favourite reasons for running an online business?**

Freedom is number one. It's the freedom to work when I want and where I want. I run my business from my home in Osaka, from a tourist bureau counter in my old hometown in Switzerland, from a hotel room in Singapore.

I also enjoy the feeling of accomplishment. When I'm creating something for my business, it's for me. When you do that for a company, it betters them and not your situation.

I get to work with all kinds of interesting people. I have contact all over the world, who I communicate with on Skype, forums, e-mail.

24. **Any final words?**

Before somebody decides that they want to build their own business, they really need to take a close look at themselves. Are they cut out to run a business? You really need to be self-driven, self-directed, and have a bulldog persistence. You cannot go into business with an "I'll give it a try" attitude.

Be truly committed and you will succeed.

Sebastian Schertel   http://www.fit24shop.com
1. **What was your first web business?**

Health and Fitness with FitLine http://www.fit24shop.com idea: to sell high quality nutritional products only and to have people get the idea that wellness products can give you power within minutes and to share this experiences

2. **When did you start this?**

Feb-04

3. **How much time did you devote to setting this up and running it?**

The first weeks were really challenging: i had a really bad hosting company and was bound about a year to their 'service'. I also had a really bad web design software. Both did not help me very much with my online business. I tried my best to get things running but it ended in working about 3-5 hours daily for about 6-8 months. But once everything was set up and running i could cut down my working time to about 3 hours daily.

4. **How much did it cost to set up and run?**

I will concentrate on answering the online thing because everything around that could also fill another book itself. Domain registration was about 35 Euro per month (bad and expensive hosting company). Web design software was for free! (oh boy never use a free web page builder again. why? no support hardly useful difficult to set up. just a few examples) Product creation was nothing i had to do. Another person was responsible for this. I did just some online marketing and programming. Logo creation: i tried to set up an own logo and it cost me a fortune for crap. I made so much mistakes. All in all the 'getting started' part was very expensive for me.

5. **How much money did you make?**

In the first time my revenue was nearly zero. After 12 months everything went better. Today there are so many sales that i don't really know how much i earn. But it is enough to pay everything i need. ;) If i had known then what i know now i would have saved so much money and earned so much more. My learning curve was really bad.

6. **What were the biggest challenges in setting up and running this web business?**

Finding a good software and a good hosting company.

7. **What happened to the web business?**

I sold a few of my old domain names. But i still own my web business and the major sites. We had a lot of changes in website design and domain names but it is now better than ever.

8. **Please provide any URLs / screenshots or other promo literature (sales page etc.)**

http://www.fit24shop.com
http://www.praevention24.de (putting new content in it right now)

9. **What is your background? (education, hobbies etc.)**
   I have something like a bachelor degree in sales (Handelsfachwirt in german) learned hypnosis have another degree in medical wellness and worked as a salesman for a few years

10. **Did your background help with this web business in anyway ?**
    Knowing what people want and how to fulfill their needs was really helpful. It was difficult to take my one-on-one sales experience to the internet level.

11. **What did you learn from this first web business?**
    Set up an easy to use site. Provide good content high quality products and get help from experienced partners.

12. **What web businesses do you run now?**
    My health and wealth business and a few other projects. But i can't tell you right now about all of them. ;)

13. **When did you start this?**
    As above

14. **How much time did you devote to setting this up and running it?**
    As above

15. **How much did it cost to set up and run?**
    As above

16. **How much money do you make?**
    As above

17. **What were the biggest challenges in setting up and running this web business?**
    As above

18. **What are your top 5 goals for this web business?**
    Be market leader for this topic in the future (5-15 years). Have 300000 subscribers to the newsletter. Have 3-8% of my country to know our brand names. Provide useful information and products to the people. Improve the site the information and change the lifes of everybody who meets us to how it should be.

19. **What top 5 tips would you give to somebody starting a business online?**
    Get a good web design software (i recommend XSitePro for internet marketers). Get Axandras Internet Business Promoter. Get a reseller account from a hosting company instead of standard webspace and features. Do NOT spend to much time surfing the internet and buying new products that might help you in your business success. YOUR ideas have to be good and to sell the way they are. Last but not least JOIN THE WARRIOR FORUM!

20. **Do you plan to start any more web businesses in the next 24 months?**
    If so, what are the details?

I have my head stuffed with new ideas. One is a website about the way our brain works.

21. What top 10 products or services would you recommend to somebody starting out online?

XSitePro. Internet Business Promoter. Opera and Firefox Browser. WarriorForum. A reliable coach. A reseller account from a good hosting company. And to stay fit and healthy (and to have the ability to work til 3 a.m.) our products. (Get them you will never regret it. Guaranteed www.fit24shop.com) ;)

22. Do you have any role models or mentors? If so, who are they, and how did you get them?

Role Models: Eikichi Onizuka (GTO) a famous japanese teacher. Robbie Williams (english singer) has a great appearance. Harald Schmidt (german entertainer). Mentor: a very good friend of mine in sales business (he is about 20 years older and much more experienced).

23. What are you top 3 favourite reasons for running an online business?

I hate doing things i don't like and going to work 10 hours a day (which i did usually) is something i don't like. Running an online business allows me to work from 9 a.m. to 12 p.m. if i like. It is flexible. I have way more influence on the lives of people when using the internet. I do not like PCs but i like to create something. To develop MY idea and watch it grow and get response from users. That really feels great.

24. Any final words?

When starting an online business. Do research. Get information. Read the forums and don't buy every crap. Tell your idea a few people that you can trust - and trust their opinion. Don't be sad if a few friends tell you they don't like your idea or it won't work. Check the facts. Be realistic. And dream. And fulfill your dream. But start part-time. And define a budget you are able to spend for software and monthly costs. If you have a good idea the right products and are willing to fulfill your dream - nobody can stop you. And you will get way more help online than you actually think. God bless you.

Index

Note

4841027

Made in the USA
Lexington, KY
07 March 2010